Christmas '89

RUGBY IS A FUNNY GAME

RUGBY IS A FUNNY GAME

Have You Heard the One About the Scotsman, the Englishman, the Irishman and the Welshman?

Gordon Brown, Andy Ripley, Fergus Slattery and Bobby Windsor

Illustrations by Jake Tebbit

STANLEY PAUL

London Melbourne Auckland Johannesburg

First published in 1987 by Stanley Paul and Co. Ltd

An imprint of Century Hutchinson Ltd

Brookmount House, 62–65 Chandos Place
Covent Garden, London WC2N 4NW

Century Hutchinson Australia (Pty) Ltd
PO Box 496, 16–22 Church Street, Hawthorn, Melbourne, Victoria 3122

Century Hutchinson New Zealand Limited
PO Box 40–086, Glenfield, Auckland 10

Century Hutchinson South Africa (Pty) Ltd
PO Box 337, Bergvlei 2012, South Africa

Set in Linotron Century by Input Typesetting Ltd, London

Printed and bound in Great Britain by
Anchor Brendon Ltd, Tiptree, Essex

British Library Cataloguing In Publication Data

Rugby is a funny game : have you heard the
one about the Scotsman, the Englishman, the
Irishman and the Welshman?
1. Rugby football—Anecdotes, facetiae,
satire, etc.
I. Brown, Gordon, *1947–*
796.33'3'0207   GV945.2

ISBN 0 09 171470 2

To all the rugby people
who are in danger of
taking the game
too seriously!

CONTENTS

INTRODUCTION

'Remember the time when . . .?' 'Whatever really happened during . . .?' 'Who was it that nearly . . .?' 'I'll never forget the player that. . . .'

It was the wee small hours of the morning in an hotel in central London and the rugby dinner had long since ended. The beer was flowing and, *as always*, Andy Ripley, Fergus Slattery, Bobby Windsor and myself were regaling each other like a machine-gun spitting bullets with the many humorous incidents and anecdotes of this magnificent game of ours — RUGBY! We were sore laughing.

Every time we were in each other's company, this always happened! 'Why don't we put some of these down in black and white for posterity?' I asked the other three. 'Great idea,' said Bobby. 'Too many serious rugby books around anyway,' said Rips. 'High time the lighter side of the game was highlighted,' said Slatts. 'Tally ho!' we all shouted, clamouring for our pens.

Following my own doctor's examination of the manuscript of this book, I can modestly advise you of his prescription for prospective readers: *Dosage* no more than ten pages four times a day. *Warning* possible side-effects include splitting sides, belly aches and crying. *Target* complete the full book to obtain maximum relief!

Gordon Brown
Troon, 1987

1
SUPERSTITIOUS NONSENSE

Since I began taking off my clothes with groups of men and putting on a pair of short trousers and a striped shirt, prior to going out to some muddy field to get beaten up, I've noticed something. The people I do it with are odd.

For example, the captain of Rosslyn Park, Simon Henderson, previously of Durham University. I've always taken him to be a straightforward, normal, run-of-the-mill, you-hit-me-I'll-hit-you prop-forward. He has a nice mum and has always seemed to me to be the sort of person who eventually pays his electricity bill.

Perhaps, to an itinerant fly on the wall, his pre-match dressing-room team talks may seem a little unusual – the long silence, and agitated jumping up and down, then an order to the whole team to run on the spot and deliver a communal shout up to five. The process is repeated and then everyone hits each other and this is followed by a question and answer session. Simon shouts at the top of his voice, 'What are we going to do?' Simon is not expecting a reasoned response about the future of mankind. No, the assembled sweating and now slightly bruised players have to shout back, even louder, 'Win.' Far from being unusual, this is part of a well-laid-down rite performed in thousands of dressing rooms all over the country on any Saturday afternoon between about 2.45 and 2.55.

What is strange, though, is what Simon does before he jumps, screams, punches people and leads the communal chanting: he puts one of his Rosslyn Park rugby football socks on – inside out. Not that strange, you may say. However, consider this: every time he plays he knowingly and quite deliberately, wears one sock inside out, and even more importantly he doesn't tell anyone.

Now, compared to eating a world-record number of raw eggs, this may not be a mind-bogglingly bizarre activity, but a question does arise: why does he do it?

He is not alone.

In the same room over many years I have regularly fallen over one Nicholas 'Gonzo' Anderson, formerly captain of Surrey and Birmingham University 2nd XV. Gonzo has a big mortgage on a very small house in Wimbledon, is a failed windsurfer and likes drinking Carlsberg Special Brew. Also, when he runs out onto the pitch, he has to cross every line, except the broken ten-yard line, with his left foot first. In the highly unlikely event of Rosslyn Park scoring a try, when he runs back again he has to put his left foot onto each line other than the broken ten-yard line. He always makes sure when he runs onto the pitch before the game starts, and before he starts stepping on lines, that he is the thirteenth player to leave the dressing room. He is, of course, nuts. Why does he do it? He is not alone. I believe every single player in the team is wrapped up in some personal mumbo-jumbo. Whether it's leaving the dressing room first or last or next to last, getting dressed or undressed in some special way, each one is involved in some secret rite. It is something special to do with Rosslyn Park? No. They are not alone.

They are all at it. I played rugby for twelve years with the very wonderful Big Neil Mantell, who weighed 16 stone and was 6 foot 4 inches tall at birth. His mum never forgave him. I never in all those twelve years suspected that he too was a closet weirdo. I now find out that Neil, whether playing for Rosslyn Park, Nottingham, England or whoever, when doing the good old communal stretching routine in the dressing room – roll your shoulders, stretch your hamstrings, touch your left foot – always does these exercises in groups of seven. 'Roll your arms above your head, five times,' says the dressing-room martinet. Neil does it seven times. What's up? Can't Neil add? He's rumoured to be an accountant. Still, I've always suspected accountants couldn't do sums. 'Do ten trunk curls.' Neil does seven.

Probably the best known of the many dressing-room mumbo-jumboists is the former Irish full-back, Roddy O'Donnell, a 1983 lion who played many times for Ireland and was fresh out of Ulster. I never met Roddy, but his reputation was immense, largely because the guy lumbered himself with a whole series of bizarre rituals.

Roddy would only go out onto the pitch once. No problem with that, it would seem. You only have to go out once to play; in fact, it would be difficult for anyone other than a physical schizophrenic to go out twice. In international matches, however, you go out to have the team photo taken, then you go back into the dressing room to beat your team mates up, then you come out to play the game. For those of you, like Neil Mantell, who can't count, that's twice. I don't think Roddy O'Donnell featured in too many of the Irish team photographs.

Another of Roddy's obsessions was unfortunately obvious, even to my wife, who knows less about rugby than my one-year-old daughter. When the opposition scored a try and then the opposing goal kicker converted the try. Roddy would have to gather the ball so he could run to the posts and throw it back over the crossbar and catch it on the other side of the bar. He'd then give the ball back to his stand-off so the game could continue. He tried to carry out this little strategy nonchalantly, as if it were a perfectly normal thing to do. In fact, Roddy's customs need a whole book to themselves. He was advised to stop playing rugby when he broke his neck.

One particular player in a team, who usually surrounds himself with a whole load of excess baggage is the guy who takes the penalty kicks and conversions – usually but not always the full-back. Before the match he might go out of the dressing room to practise his kicking according to some ritualized format. Three attempts from the right, two from the left and one from the middle, or whatever. He might make a point of *not* practising before a match. Often there is a maker's name on the ball: some kickers like the name always turned towards them, some facing away from them, some like it to be the right way up so the first letter is near the ground or maybe the wrong way up so the last letter is nearest the ground . . . . Then there's the run up. When players used laced-up rugby balls, then the positioning of the lace had some rationality about it; this I can fully appreciate. However, you talk to the man who takes the place kicks about his run-up when he's in mellow mood and feeling weak and vulnerable and you'll find out that his unique style of run-up has little to do with rationality and everything to do with mumbo-jumbo.

So why do so many players burden themselves with all sorts of strange rituals, and why is the place kicker the most susceptible, other than the really brick-short-of-a-load Roddy-clone?

In a game of rugby the difference between winning and losing is usually very marginal. You need everything going for you. You can train as hard as you like individually and collectively as a team. You can do everything just right. So when the whistle goes to start the game you've put yourself in a position to win. But there is still a major uncertainty about the future. You need good fortune.

That's why players need to take out the bit in the corner by wearing one sock inside out, treading on particular lines, etc., etc.

The difference between success and failure is most marked in the goal kicker. That's why his ritual is usually even more highly developed and secretive than other players. If he kicks the ball over the crossbar and through the posts, he's a hero; if he fails, he is something less.

Rugby has no monopoly on superstitious rituals, good luck charms, etc. The kicker in an American Professional Football Team gets not only instant adulation or criticism from his whole world, but his livelihood depends on immediate success. The finalists in the Olympic 100 metres know that a tenth of a second may be the difference between being Mr Inter-galactic Hero and Nowhere Man. Those guys must be loaded down with ritual and bits of 'special' clobber.

It is, of course, absolutely and totally ridiculous that sane rational individuals resort to taking comfort in wearing lucky ties, jackets, trousers, shirts, etc., or following certain stylized courses of action.

Such practices are in no way comparable to what happened to me in 1984 before the Hong Kong seven-a-side championship, when I was seated next to Mrs Purves at a pre-match function at the Hong Kong and Shanghai Bank, the joint sponsors of the competition. Now Mrs Purves, married to, would you believe, Mr Purves, a major wheel in the aforesaid banking institution, talked to me about how Hong Kong was, in the world of uncertainty and superstition, the capital city of the planet. She then told me that her lucky number was five. Now, I don't know why but I've always liked five as well, and from that day to this I know that five is just fine. I also knew that on the following day I, playing at prop (number 3), would *have* to wear the number 5 shirt.

Before returning to the following day, I'd to tell you about lumbering yourself with a 'lucky' number.

Every morning when I wake up I ask myself what day is it. Let's say it's 23 October 1988. Well, the year 1988 is a good year, because 1 plus 9 makes 10, and 8 minus 8 is 0, so as 10 divides by 5 it's gotta be a good year. The month of October, although there are seven letters in its name, is in fact the tenth month, and, as we know, 10 is divisible by 5 – terrific month. The date is the 23rd – well, that's easy, 2 plus 3 makes 5 – it's gonna be a great day. In fact, you've only got to find one 5-related number in a date to make it OK. You may say the guy is as nutty as Roddy but *I'm* just grateful my lucky number isn't 417,382. Actually, 4 plus 1 plus 7 plus 3 plus 8 plus 2 adds up to 25, which is of course 5 × 5 – pretty lucky, don'tcha think?

Everywhere I look I'm adding up, subtracting, multiplying, dividing.

My wife is Austrian, so I spend a bit of time sitting in ski lifts in her home village. Each chair is numbered, so, instead of relaxing and looking at the scenery, I'm working out what number seat I am sitting in and whether it can be related to 5 and as a consequence whether I shall be OK.

Back to Mrs Purves and Hong Kong . . . Oh – there is one other thing I should tell you.

In the early eighties there was a sports-related TV programme called 'Superstars' which I competed in. The three things most people remember about this programme are: Kevin Keegan falling off his bike, tearing the skin off his back and getting back on again; Brian Jacks eating oranges; and Sonny Liston drowning in a swimming pool. Anyway, during these programmes I found that if I used the red lane or wore red then I did rather well. I did some UK heats, a UK final, an international final and then the world final, and every time I wore red I did well. It followed that red was my lucky colour: yet more garbage to hang around my neck, along with the albatross of 5.

Actually, I've always enjoyed playing for Rosslyn Park (broad red and white hooped shirts). I've enjoyed but always felt less confident playing for Middlesex (thin blue and white shirts and blue socks). It is also no surprise to me that Wales (red shirts) and France (red socks) have always done rather well at the expense of Scotland (blue) Ireland (green) and England (white). England have done well on tour, but that of course was due to the red rose on the white shirt.

So, back to Mrs Purves and Hong Kong. I was at that time, because I was the eldest in the team, captain of the Public School Wanderers. The Public School Wanderers have a very nice red stripe on their shirts and

there I was running out in shirt number 5. Huw Davis, the stand-off, natural owner of the number 5 shirt, now wearing number 3, thought I was nutty but didn't say too much. I think he was wearing one sock up and one down at the time and stepping on unbroken lines three times with his left foot and twice with his right.

Anyway, the combination of the red stripe in the shirt and me wearing number 5 worked: we got through to the semi-finals. Good old Mrs Purves.

However, hidden forces were at work. In the team at scrum-half, on loan from Cardiff central jail, was David Bishop. Now Bish does all these strange things. I can't understand it myself. Why isn't he normal like the rest of us? One of them is that his mum has to cross him with holy water before a game. When he's playing in Pontypool, this is easy enough. Now, if Bish is in Hong Kong and his mum is in Pontypool, this would normally present a problem. Not, however, to the resourceful Dave. Thinking ahead, he'd packed a bottle of the holy water. Unfortunately, come the semi-final against Fiji, he'd either lost it or used it up: in spite of the red stripe and the number 5, we lost to Fiji 6–12. Next time Dave will just have to bring a bigger bottle. *(A.R.)*

'Well, the year 1988 is a good year, because 1 plus 9 makes 10, and 8 minus 8 is 0, so as 10 divides by 5, it's gotta be a good year.'

2

FRENCH PRANKS

One year I flew with the Glasgow rugby XV to Toulouse in the South of France. Toulouse is in the centre of the rugby hotbed of France and despite having many internationals in the Glasgow XV we were nevertheless a bit apprehensive about the game. However, the press had assured us that we would get a wonderful reception, and that no doubt we would play in front of a capacity crowd of about 30,000. When we landed at Toulouse airport I was first out of the plane and I couldn't believe the vast crowds who were thronging the airport terminal building. The open-air public terraces were literally swarming with people, all cheering and waving. My immediate reaction was 'Bloody hell this is incredible.' I knew they took their rugby seriously in that part of the country but this was crazy. As I walked down the steps of the aeroplane I started to wave back to them and the thought ran through my head: 'This is the real Big Time, Gordon.'

I reached the bottom of the steps – and there, amid the commotion, was Concorde about to take off on its maiden flight.   (G.B.)

In 1971 I made my first visit to Paris with the Scottish rugby team. On the Thursday evening before the match we visited one of Paris's famous night spots, the Folies Bergères. One of the highlights of the show, which features many semi-naked young ladies, is when the chief hostess invites one person from each country to come up on to the stage to demonstrate how a person of that nationality kisses a young lady. Being the youngest

'... there was Concorde about to take off on its maiden flight.'

member of the Scottish team, I was duly pushed forward by everyone to represent Scotland. I took my position on stage along with about a dozen others. The hostess came right down the line being kissed by every one of us, and I did my piece for my country! Lo and behold I was awarded first prize. Everyone was sent from the stage except for myself, and the girl then told me that she was going to demonstrate how the French girls like to kiss a young man. I did not notice in my excitement that she had caked herself with about two inches of lipstick on each lip. As the roars from my team-mates in the front stalls rang in my ear I awaited her attentions. She proceeded to kiss me all round my face, each kiss extremely exaggerated. Covering me with large lip smacks, she worked her way, amid a crescendo of noise from the audience, towards her finale, the mouth-to-mouth smacker – which was rather a disappointment, though I enjoyed the overall performance. Amid my team-mates' cheers I took my seat again. On our way back to the hotel after the show we looked into a café for some coffee and sandwiches before putting our heads down for the night. Whereupon one of the employees of the café looked at me, they said, 'Ah, you have been to the Folies Bergères.' News travels fast here, I thought. *(G.B.)*

On my first visit to Paris I was naturally eager to explore the night life, especially on the Saturday night following the game. The seasoned campaigners told me I would need a lot of money because Paris was the most expensive city in Europe. However, my brother Peter said to me, 'Keep your eyes on the French team after the international dinner and when they move out follow them onto their team bus.' I obeyed his instructions, and found myself at the back of their bus attempting to converse with the French team in my Ayrshire schoolboy pigeon French, which somehow narrowly failed to break the language barrier. It mattered not a jot. The bus was just about to move off when Peter came on with their skipper, Benoit Dauga, and we set off on a trip to remember. The first stop was an enormous cinema in the heart of Paris, into which we all marched arm in arm. We danced and chanted our way down the centre aisle and up onto the stage, bringing the film to a grinding halt. The lights in the cinema came on and we all immediately started to do a high-kicking can-can, arms interlocked, singing the Marseillaise. The whole audience clapped in rhythm to our efforts and when we finished a voice boomed out over a loudspeaker that we were the victorious French

rugby team. This produced mass applause and cheering and we interlocked arms once more and danced off the stage and back up the centre
aisle. As we neared the exit the applause subsided, the audience settled
down, the lights dimmed and the picture began to roll again. Once back
on the bus I marvelled at what had just happened and reflected that if
we had done that in Glasgow the effect would have been quite different.
The clever one-liner *'C'est la vie,* Jimmy' just might not have worked in
our favour. *(G.B.)*

My brother Peter enjoyed playing rugby immensely. There was never a
dull moment when he was around. He had quite an array of trademarks:
heading the ball, cottonwool bunged up both nostrils to stem the flow of
blood from his regular nosebleeds, enormous reverse cross-field passes,
turning his back on balls he was just about to kick over the bar (he
turned his back on the ball, he said, because he liked to take it by
surprise), and the amazing flight trajectory of his goal kicks. One kick
at the Stade Colombes stadium in Paris dipped, curled, tumbled and
eventually crawled almost apologetically over the bar. It was described
perfectly in the *Scotsman* newspaper on the Monday morning by Norman
Mair: 'a ballistic miracle.' *(G.B.)*

On the morning of a France–Scotland international in Paris a London/
Scottish XV was playing against a local junior side. On the previous
night the London/Scottish boys had been partaking of the local *vin* and
every single one of them had had far too much to drink. However this
did not seem to upset their game plan: they were winning all the balls
and scoring all the tries against the local team despite the previous
night's excesses. With ten minutes to go, and after their having won
every single scrum in the whole game no matter who put the ball in, a
scrum was given to London/Scottish only ten yards from the opposition
goal line. It was here that their chickens came home to roost. The London/
Scottish scrum-half put the ball into the scrum – and the London/Scottish
loosehead was sick all over the ball. As the London/Scottish hooker
hesitated before striking the sick-sodden object back through the scrum
to the number 8, the voice of D. K. Smith, the number 8, boomed out:
'Good ball to lose, Scottish!' *(G.B.)*

The prelude to all France–Wales matches held in the Parc des Princes in Paris is the hair-raising bus ride from the team's hotel to the ground itself. With two police outriders in front, the team coach, followed by the committee coach, goes at a minimum speed of sixty miles per hour right through the centre of Paris, crashing every red light en route. During my last visit, in 1975, one Frenchman in a small Renault car unfortunately positioned himself between the two buses not long after our leaving the team's hotel . . . . As the pace hotted up, it became apparent that he couldn't get past the front bus, and couldn't slow down because of the bus behind. Trapped like this for the entire journey, he eventually arrived at the Parc des Princes with his eyes standing out of his head and perspiring heavily. It wasn't where he had intended to go, but it was better than being the filling in a bus sandwich.   *(B.W.)*

3

AUCHTER-COCKALEEKIE

I was once invited to a rugby club in Yorkshire of which John Spencer, the great England three-quarter and captain, was a member. The match was a challenge between the Upper Wharfedale Ist XV and an invitation international XV. John Taylor, the Welsh and British Lions wing-forward, was the captain of the international team and was also leading the pack. He was calling the line-out codes. My second-row partners that night were Geoff Evans, the London Welsh player, and Delme Thomas from Neath. The line-out codes were very simple: if a Scottish town was called, the ball was to go to me at number 8; if an English town was called, the ball was to go to Geoff Evans; and if a Welsh town was called, the ball was to go to Delme. Things went very well indeed until midway through the second half, when John Taylor could not remember the name of any Scottish towns and he particularly wanted the ball thrown to me. After a few moments' hesitation he shouted out to all and sundry, 'Auchtercockaleekie.' The ball was duly thrown to me.   *(G.B.)*

During a match played at Ayr between Ayr and Jordanhill the front-row confrontation was quite intense and two of the props in particular, Jock Craig of Ayr and Struan McCallum of Jordanhill, were having an almighty battle which was getting a bit out of hand. Eventually the referee, Alan Hosie, who was later to become an international referee, grabbed both Craig and McCallum, led them fully twenty yards away from the rest of the players and said to them, 'If you two want to have such a torrid time on your own, why don't you just go round behind that stand and carry on with your own wee game and leave us here to get on with the game that really matters?' Craig said to Hosie, 'Well, there is only one problem if we do that.' 'What's that?' 'We know who the crowd would follow!'   *(G.B.)*

Jock Craig, the Ayr prop, was immensely strong. It was said that on his farm, when he was called upon to bring in the bull, scorning the great long pole with the hook on the end, he simply got a hold of the bull by the nose and led it quietly into its pen. There was a time when Jock's bull would not go to the cows as normal so Jock headed for the vet. The vet asked, 'Didn't we have a problem with this bull some years ago?' To which Jock replied, 'Yes, and at that time you gave me some pills to administer to the bull and they worked a treat.' The vet scratched his head. 'Mm. Unfortunately I've had some flood damage here and my records are not up to date. Can you describe the pills to me?' 'They were large orange pills,' said Jock, 'with sort of black speckles on them.' The vet said, 'Well, that could describe quite a number of pills. Can't you be more specific?' 'Well,' said Jock, 'they had a wee bit of a pepperminty taste to them.'   *(G.B.)*

When I was first picked to play for Scotland, my brother Peter, who had been capped a few times by then, said to me, 'Don't be nervous before the match. All you'll have to think about is the fabulous feeling of running down the tunnel at Murrayfield.' When the day arrived and I entered the dressing room my heart was already beating fifty to the dozen, and the nearer the kick-off got the more excited I became, but nevertheless I calmed myself with the thought of running down the tunnel. Eventually the blood and thunder of the captain's team talk was finished and the steward summoned us to the top of the tunnel to follow the opposition, the Springboks, down onto the field. As we stood at the top of the tunnel, I looked right down across the pitch to the far side, where I could see the crowd with the Lion Rampant flags flying in the wind. The pipe band with at least fifty pipers was standing on the turf playing 'Scotland the Brave', and the sound of this was wafting up the tunnel towards us. By this time my excitement pitch meant that my heart was beating a hundred to the dozen; eventually the steward let us go and we set off down the tunnel. I do not know if I had ever felt as proud in my life before. The further down the tunnel I ran the bigger I seemed to get, and I remember thinking halfway down the tunnel, 'I'm never going to get out that wee hole at the bottom.' *(G.B.)*

There was a time when Peter and I were vying with each other for the same position in the Scottish rugby team. We were all eagerly awaiting the announcement of the team to play Wales at Cardiff Arms Park. Some of the newspapers had suggested that both the Brown brothers might be selected. I was waiting in my office for a phone call from the press man who always seemed to get the team before everyone else. Someone in the office shouted to me, 'Broonie, that's a call to do with the Scottish rugby team,' so I rushed across and picked up the phone. It was not the pressman but my big brother, Peter, and he was screaming excitedly down the phone, 'Great news! Great news! I'm back in the Scottish team.' I said, 'Super! Who's out?' He said, 'You are.' *(G.B.)*

I was once playing for my club, West of Scotland, against Hutchie Grammar FP in Glasgow. Next to the Hutchie rugby pitch there was a cemetery. Midway through the second half one of the West players kicked the ball for touch and the ball flew straight into the middle of the cemetery. One of the wags in the crowd immediately shouted, 'Dead ball!' *(G.B.)*

When Terry Cobner, the Pontypool and Wales wing-forward, made his first visit to Murrayfield to play against Scotland the game was only two minutes old when he fell on a loose ball in the middle of the field; the ruck that followed saw not only the ball emerge behind the Scottish forwards but Terry along with it. After the game I asked him about the incident and his comment was, 'Broonie, I bear no malice. In fact, I was really impressed.' Now that is what I call a rugby fanatic. *(G.B.)*

Peter and I played for Scotland over a dozen times together. After one of the internationals at Murrayfield, as I left the dressing rooms to board the team bus, I was greeted by a wee boy who said that he had been waiting there in the rain specially to get my autograph. He was the only one left from the great throng who had earlier been pouncing on my more punctual team-mates for their autographs. He was wet and cold and he implored me to sign my autograph on his sodden match programme despite all the shouts of 'Hurry up, Broonie,' from the team bus. As I

peeled the pages open he said to me, 'You were magnificent today. Brilliant in the line-out and brilliant in the loose. In fact, you were the best player on the field.' Proudly I was just about to sign when he blurted out, 'Keep it up, Peter.' I humbly moved my pen away from my photo to Peter's and reluctantly signed *P. C. Brown*. I like to think that made him happy . . . though I have to confess I wasn't actually best pleased myself!
(G.B.)

In a match between Marr FP and Ayr, one of the Ayr players got the ball kicked full in his face and it knocked him out. As he lay on his back on the ground, his daughter spied him from nearby. She turned to her friend and said, 'Oh, no! Daddy's drunk again.' *(G.B.)*

During a rugby match at Troon between Marr and Ayr one of the ball boys consistently took his time to retrieve the ball. A visiting player was rather vexed at this and told the wee boy to get his skates on in future. The wee boy then said, 'But I can't do that. My daddy will give me a row if I hurry because he's got to get as big a rest as possible.' *(G.B.)*

The All Blacks played Scotland at Murrayfield one year, and in the second row that day a young Scot called Erle Mitchell was winning his first cap. He had the daunting task of marking the legendary Colin Meads. At the first line-out, Meads thumped Mitchell. The whole crowd saw what happened. That evening Mitchell's university mates asked him how he reacted. 'I didn't mess about,' claimed Mitchell. 'At the next line-out I told Meads exactly where to go and what to do, in the most vivid Anglo-Saxon.' He paused as his fans gasped in admiration before adding, 'But I issued my threat in such a quiet whisper that unless Meads could lipread I doubt he appreciated the full force of my fury.' *(G.B.)*

I was certainly very proud when I learned that I had been picked to play for Scotland for the first time – I was to face the South African tourists at Murrayfield. The day after the team announcement was made, a note was passed round Marr College in Troon, my old school, by the rector, declaring a half-day holiday in honour of my selection. There was very

'I humbly moved my pen away from my photo to Peter's and reluctantly signed P. C. Brown.'

little chance of such instant fame going to my head. It was reported to
me that evening that, on hearing the good news, one boy immediately
stood on his desk in the classroom and, punching the air with his fists,
uttered the words, 'Three cheers for Gordon Brown . . . whoever the hell
he is.'   *(G.B.)*

Referees have always kept a weather eye on Gala scrum-half Dunky
Paterson. Something in the cut of his jib seems to arouse their suspicions,
even if he hasn't done anything. The Scottish touring team were
returning from Argentina one year, trundling through the 'Nothing to
Declare' gate at Heathrow airport with their bags and trollies; of the
twenty-five of us, only one was stopped – Dunky Paterson. He really
didn't have anything to declare, and was eventually allowed to rejoin us
after a good frisking. The following year, the Scottish team again found
itself in the arrivals lounge at Heathrow, this time having come home
from Australia. Once again, all twenty-five players were shuffling
through the 'Nothing to Declare' gate, when suddenly a customs official
waved one of us over. Dunky Paterson again! Now, I'm not suggesting
that Customs and Excise are in cahoots with the rugby referees, but next
time you're at Heathrow airport check if the famous red and green signs
have been changed – you'll know why. The green sign will read, 'Nothing
to Declare', and the red one will say, 'Goods to Declare – and Dunky
Paterson'.   *(G.B.)*

In the late sixties and early seventies the captain at West of Scotland
was Quintin Dunlop, the club hooker. Quintin was one of the greatest
rugby enthusiasts I have ever met and was constantly introducing to the
team new and exciting moves. He also introduced a competition whereby
every week he would award each team member points for certain categ-
ories – the number of times you turned up at training, the effort you put
into training, how well you played each Saturday, how much effort you
put into each Saturday, etc. Each subject on his list started at 6 points
and worked its way down to 1. During one of our matches in Edinburgh
against Melville College FP my second-row partner was Colin Payne, the
English international. The longer the game went on the more points we
scored, and we were bringing out all of Quintin's favourite moves. As the
points mounted up, all of us began to realize that there were many
points for each individual going begging in this game as far as Quintin's

personal points league was concerned. With about ten minutes to go this fact finally dawned on Colin Payne; as he had been taking it rather easily in the second half, he knew he would have to do something to gain good favour with Quintin. The game had only two minutes to go when, following a magnificent move from one end of the field to the other, the final pass saw Colin running over between the posts; but, instead of touching the ball down for a try, he stood two yards over the opposition's line and holding the ball aloft shouted, 'Quintin, Quintin, Quintin. Where are you?' As Colin is 6 foot 6, when he was standing holding the ball aloft, none of the small guys in the opposition near him could reach the ball! Eventually he spied Quintin and threw the ball to him. Quintin duly caught it and dived over the line to score the try. We all said, 'Colin, what the hell were you playing at?' He quickly smiled and replied, 'That pass *has* to be worth 6 points – to me!' *(G.B.)*

In the early seventies the Scottish rugby team coach was Bill Dickinson. Following a very tough and physical Sunday squad session at Murrayfield taken by Bill, we hauled ourselves back to the dressing room. We were so exhausted that no one seemed to have the energy even to strip off to have a shower. However, undaunted as usual, big Al McHarg was soon lathering himself under the shower, and when Bill entered the dressing room to survey the scene he realized that big Al was the only one in motion. 'Well, well,' said Bill, 'would you look at Adonis in there.' Big Al's reply was immediate: 'What do you mean, *A* donis? *The* ruddy donis!' *(G.B.)*

The Scottish stand-off in the early seventies was Ian Robertson of Watsonians. At that particular time Ian was an English lecturer at Fettes College in Edinburgh. Fettes is one of the better known private boys' schools in Scotland and Ian was very proud of the fact that he was working there. On the eve of an international he was telling us everything we'd ever wanted to know about Fettes and quite a lot we didn't. My attention began to wander. Calling to mind a two-day rugby seminar, at Fettes, I had attended from my own school, Marr College in Troon, I thought, 'I know how to put a stop to this'. 'I went to Fettes College,' I said, butting into the monologue. 'Oh yes,' he retorted, 'and what were you doing – delivering the milk?' *(G.B.)*

In 1983, during the All Blacks tour of the UK, they played against a Glasgow XV in Glasgow. With fifteen minutes of the game to go, one of the New Zealand forwards was injured and had to be substituted. The All Blacks substitute was none other than Andy Haden, who stands 6 foot 8 and weighs 19 stone – a colossus of a man. He made his way down from the stand at the Hughenden ground in Glasgow, came out onto the pitch and peeled off his All Blacks tracksuit. A line-out was waiting to be taken to recommence the game. As Haden walked across, he towered above every single person on the field. Just as he was stepping out onto the pitch, a Scots voice from the stand shouted out, 'Haw, All Blacks, that's no' fair – wan only!'   *(G.B.)*

It was one of the matches in which Peter and I both played for Scotland against the All Blacks. We were three points adrift from the All Blacks. There was only a few minutes remaining and we were battering at their goal line, trying to get the winning score. The ball was touched down behind their line for a drop-out twenty-five. All the Scottish forwards went across and we were gathered near the touchline in front of the old stand. The All Black stand-off had the ball ready to take the drop kick. The noise coming from the old stand was unbelievable but above this Peter shouted to me from about twelve yards infield, 'If it is a high hanging ball I'll headie it and you run on to it.' Not many people who play rugby realize that you are allowed to headie the ball, and those who do know are not daft enough to try it. *I knew Peter meant it.* But he had no sooner shouted this than the All Blacks stand-off turned round and thumped the ball away up the park. As we turned to run back to cover, Peter shouted over his shoulder to me, 'The bugger must have heard me.'
(G.B.)

On another occasion Scotland were playing Australia at Murrayfield. It was not the strongest Australian touring side, but their hooker Peter Horton was a little devil and he spent the whole game causing trouble. One particular incident with only two minutes to go left a bitter taste in our mouths, but despite all our efforts throughout the game we had been unable to quell his vigour! At the international dinner that night I was sitting opposite him at the table. The wine was flowing and the patter

'. . . he towered above every single person in the field.'

was rolling. At the end of the dinner, when all the players stood up on the chairs to sing 'Auld Lang Syne', I had to stand half on the table and half on the chair to link up with Peter. As we swayed to and fro, I unfortunately lost my balance and fell backwards over my chair, pulling him down on top of me. As he fell, his head struck the top table. He landed on top of me and rolled under the top table unconscious. I quickly dived under the top table after him, followed by three or four of my team-mates, and as we splashed his face with water and tried gently to bring him round I burst out laughing. My team-mates said to me, 'Broonie, why do you find this funny?' I remarked, 'Well, just look at us . . . only a few hours ago concern for *him* was the last thing on our minds!'

(G.B.)

During my three months' suspension following my sending-off incident, in order to get as fit as possible prior to my return to the game I started training with the Glasgow Rangers Football Club, whose manager at that time was the one and only Jock Wallace. Now Jock was renowned for his horrific training schedules and he certainly put me through the mill. He also, however, had a name for being caring and knowing how to treat his players properly. One day Jock was giving me a real workout at Ibrox Park. The climax had me sprinting all the way to the top of the steep terracing. I was to do it ten times but after seven I was shattered and told him that I could not do any more. He quietly said to me, 'Is that so? We'll see.' After one minute's rest he took my pulse and then ordered me to the top of the terracing once again. I managed it, but only just. This time he gave me two minutes' rest, and after taking my pulse sent me off again. I managed eventually to reach the top. I was absolutely knackered. I could scarcely breathe. I was dizzy. My body was racked with pain. Jock's booming voice brought tears to my eyes. 'Only one to go, Broonie!' I did not think I would be able to go *down* the terracing, never mind come back up it again. However, after two more minutes, I set off again. It was agony. He was behind me barking at my heels. I had to make it to the top. I just had to. My lungs, head, arms and legs were bursting. Eventually I made it. I hung over a crush barrier and vomited. My stomach wretched five or six times. I thought I was going to die. I just wanted to be left alone hanging there to die in peace. Jock came across to me and he said, 'Bloody good, son, now come away inside before you catch a wee chill.'

(G.B.)

I was preparing to open my new building society office in Glasgow and as usual there was the last-minute rush of painters, carpet fitters, joiners, etc. Eventually, on the last afternoon before the opening, everyone had finished and cleared out of the office except one joiner who was left to put up six important company photographs on my wall. At 4.59 p.m., with three of the pictures up and three still to go, I saw him putting on his jacket and making for the door, obviously *en route* for the nearest pub. I quickly headed him off at the door and said, 'Hey, hang on a moment, pal – do you know how many people will be coming into this office at nine o'clock tomorrow morning? I will tell you . . . fifty.' 'Wrong, pal,' he replied. 'There will be fifty-one.' With that, our dedicated clock watcher disappeared into the night. *(G.B.)*

In 1985 there was a Rumanian rugby referee on an exchange visit in Wales. During one match a second-row forward was indulging in a bit of skulduggery, and the Rumanian referee, although not having much command of the English language, was able to get over to this player the message 'any more and you are off'. The forwards were not enamoured of this referee because he was not doing very well, and the second-row forward who had earlier been warned continued with his skulduggery. After some time the referee called him over and, pointing to the pavilion, said, 'Offskie! Offskie!' The Welsh player started to walk away, mumbling exactly what he thought of the referee. On hearing this, the Rumanian retorted, 'Ze apology is too late.' *(B.W.)*

4

WEST NORFOLK FARMERS RFC 2ND XV

I was twenty-one when I heard that song,
I'm thirty-nine now but I won't be for long.
Knees that were strong, fall apart.

The collection of stuff in this – for want of a better word – book most of us grew out of around the time of puberty. It is, however, aimed at raising a rugby-related snigger. Nothing wrong with a snigger. Four million people read the *Sun* and they can't all be wrong. Or can they?

The real laugh of course, is that Bobby, Gordon, Fergus and I are in fact the butt of nature's joke. As probably, old bean, are you. Nature is a great joker; eventually she kills us.

When I was a child of twenty summers I imagined that it all went on for ever. Now, at almost forty, I know it doesn't.

I'm still playing, but the change from mobile young thruster to crumbling pillar of the establishment seems to have happened so suddenly. The sun glistened on the window and then, blink, here I am, crows' feet around the eyes and an inability to run the 400 metres hurdles in under 60 seconds. I'm afraid to blink again. I might not wake up.

Still, I must have learned something in those twenty years. Actually, learning is not only to do with time serving; it is probably to do with something else, I'm not too sure what. Before I creep up on my own semantic backside, let me tell you about my first years playing rugby –

even though they don't amount to a bag of beans, except to me. Let's hear it for self-indulgence. Let it roll 10–4.

Well. Aged nineteen. Summer 1966. There I was, too big to play soccer, too short to play basketball, too fast to win a slow bicycle race, and too slow to win the 100 yards AAA final then held at the White City. But just perfect for a rugby football forward, albeit a spindly one.

Hayden Morris, sports coordinator at the University of East Anglia and ex-British Lions wing three-quarter, trawling through the 1966 intake, picked the forwards with a three-quarter's selection policy that has remained unchanged since William Webb Ellis got lazy: fatties who eat lots of buns play in the front row; beanpoles play in the second row and at number 8; and small aggressive potential bar-room brawlers play in the back row.

I don't know whether you too played against West Norfolk Farmers RFC 2nd XV in the season of 1966–67, when you were nineteen and had been playing rugby for about six weeks and were shaped like a bamboo pole weighing in at 12 stone with a predilection for listening to the Mike Cotton Ram Jam Band doing a version of the Four Tops' 'Reach Out I'll Be There'. If you were there, you'll know it was not a bunch of laughs.

For a start, I mean, I really didn't mind getting changed in an old shed. We'd played the week before against Holt RFC; on that occasion we'd also changed in a shed. Rugby players obviously get changed in sheds and then wash afterwards under a cold tap. I could live with that; my personal hygiene has always been suspect.

Neither did I mind playing on an ex-turnip-townsend-four-year-crop-rotation field. Muddy and October it may have been, but like the rest of Norfolk it was flat.

Neither was I overly concerned that I didn't know the rules and hadn't a clue what was going on. Quite frankly, I've always found that to be a definite advantage.

Again, the fact that the players in the West Norfolk Farmers 2nd XV were really old, about twenty-three, and were paying taxes so we could ponce about in beads and kaftans didn't concern me too much. Actually I've always had the feeling that there weren't any farmers in the West Norfolk Farmers 2nd XV. I think the name was a misnomer. Like those old City societies, 'The Worshipful Company of Lamplighters' – I mean, the only lamp they ever worship under is the one they use when they're

trying to work out the Inland Revenue implications of being a name at Lloyds and their resulting tax position. I digress.

So here I am: nineteen, playing a game which I didn't understand, thin as a rake, bleeding, muddy, dressed in a kaftan, talking to an old man of twenty-seven with a bent ear who half an hour earlier had tried to disembowel me. Yo, so this is rugby.

As is often the case when it seems things can't get any worse, they do. That season I progressed through Diss RFC, Lowestoft and Yarmouth RFC, and all points east of Dereham and north of Ipswich YMCA. We qualified in the UAU competition (Eastern) because Essex University RFC hadn't turned up to play; Princess Margaret was visiting the university and the players were at a demonstration against something or other while developing their critical conscience. But we later got smashed by Sussex University, whose team apparently should have been demonstrating on that particular day but unfortunately Sussex University selection committee had made a mistake and allowed in a group of itinerant South Wales rugby players who'd been locked in a 1920s' time warp. Didn't they know they should be wearing capes, listening to Donovan and reciting poetry in a Wimpy Bar – didn't they know this was 1966? Screw team sports and anything else, given half a chance. (Yes, I could make it as a tabloid features journalist.)

Then came seasons 1967–68 and 1968–69. I now weighed 14 stone, knew the rules (sort of), and North Walsham had moved from a shed to a school pitch. What's more, I had gone to find my fortune in London. Fat chance. Articled clerk living on £65 a month in a grotty attic in Notting Hill Gate.

Still, I did know where the Rosslyn Park Rugby Football Club ground was because my sister had lived nearby. So I turned up there at the end of August. The day of the trials.

I had hoped that the changing-room conditions might have been an improvement over those in Norfolk. No, Rosslyn Park was, is and probably always will be a brick-clad Nissen hut with one agriculturally exhausted playing field running twelve sides. Its big advantage is its location: people know where the ground is, so it attracts itinerants,

'... fatties who eat lots of buns play in the front row: beanpoles play in the second row.'

domestic and foreign, and embryonic fortune hunters aged twenty-one from Liverpool, brought up in Bristol and with three years' limited rugby experience gained in Norfolk.

The trial. Man in a blazer behind a desk. 'Name?' 'Andy Ripley.' 'Age?' 'Twenty-one.' 'School?' 'Greenway Comprehensive.' 'Rugby experience?' 'Three years at the University of East Anglia.' 'Position?' 'Don't mind.' 'Fine, we'll call you.' They didn't. Well, they didn't until the last game of the extras-making up the numbers. Nothing against me personally; in the late 1970s Murray Mexted played for Rosslyn Park 6th team for a season.

I got picked for the 5th XV. Some time in early September 1969, I played against Marlow 3rd XV at Marlow.

Then, by a combination of turning up and other people's misfortunes, I got the call on a Friday night on the communal telephone. 'Call for room number twelve.' Switched off the Cream, who apart from 'Badge' I never really liked, ran down two flights of communal stairs. Someone had dropped out. Could I play in the 1st XV against Richmond 1st XV? Date 6 December 1969. I could, I could, I would, I would. Excited? You bet I was. Stuck all day at Shell Mex house for two months, doing the schedule for a debtors' circularization, letters M to R. Long-standing girlfriend given me the elbow. Room-mate launching himself into the world of heavy dope.

I was at Roehampton early. Most rugby players in Rosslyn Park in the 1st XV in 1969 hadn't played the chameleon so they had blazers and ties and had missed out on affected scruffiness. Who cared? There I was with Geoff Bayles, John Stafford and John Nielson. Men. There I was, the new kid in town. The pre-match rites and rituals which have been a part of my life now for twenty years were new and exciting. The captain welcomed me to the side and everyone wished me all the best.

The game started. I would like to say I made a dream debut. However, I can't remember anything about the game other than that it was freezing cold, the pitch was frozen and just into the second half, when the ball was miles away, I fell over and landed heavily on my left knee. Unbeknown to me or anyone else, I had just bust my knee into five pieces. I stayed on and limped, and in the shower afterwards my knee came up like a football.

I set out on what, over twenty years, has become a familiar journey:

half a mile up Roehampton Lane to Queen Mary's Hospital. The knee was drained and X-rayed. The doctor, bless her, didn't take it off but put me in plaster and I went back to the attic. Some dream debut. Some start to the great and wonderful world of rugby. *(A.R.)*

5

DIFFERENT STROKES

In 1974, during the British Lions tour of South Africa, Gareth Edwards and I golfed regularly and it was during one of these golf matches that a press man who had followed us round asked, 'How would you like to play against Gary Player?' Not wishing to appear over-enthusiastic, we replied that that would be rather nice and we would try and fit it into our schedule. The papers then became full of the story of Gary Player about to take on Gareth and myself and it went on for weeks and weeks. Eventually a time and date was settled for the momentous occasion. Our team-mates kept pulling our legs about this great game of golf and, as excited as we were, the closer the date came the more we found it difficult to believe in. Unfortunately our fears were confirmed when, two days before the supposed game, we were told that Mr Player had been delayed in America and would be unable to keep his appointment with us. Hopefully another date might be found prior to the end of the tour. As you can imagine, Gareth and I were both very disappointed. This didn't stop one or two of our team-mates going to town by each day pulling our legs more and more about the 'game'. One of the ringleaders of this band was Bobby Windsor. During the last week of the tour the telephone in my bedroom rang and, picking it up I heard a voice saying, 'Could I speak to Mr Gordon Brown, please?' 'Who's calling?' The voice said, 'This is Mr Gary Player. I want to arrange a game of golf with him.' Suspecting that this was Bobby Windsor up to his usual tricks, I politely told him to go and get stuffed and that he had taken the joke far enough. The voice insisted that it was Gary Player and could he speak to Gordon Brown to arrange a game of golf. Whereupon I again told him, this time a bit more colourfully, to go and stuff himself.

There was some coughing and spluttering on the other end of the phone, followed by the same voice enunciating his words more carefully, as though talking to an imbecile. 'There seems to be some misunderstanding. This is Gary Player – the golfer – and I've just come back from Britain, where I won the British Open golf tournament. And I would like to play against Mr Gordon Brown and Mr Gareth Edwards. Sadly, I let them down earlier in the tour.' As he continued, the thought occurred to me: my God, I've underestimated Bobby Windsor's talent. The man is incredible. Why is he wasting his time playing Welsh hooker when he could be making Mike Yarwood's money? The South African accent is fantastic, and he certainly seems to know a lot about Player's schedule . . . . A horrible chill crept up my legs and then up my spine towards my neck. When it reached my brain I acted quick as a flash. I dropped the phone, did a few stamping noises, picked up the phone and said, 'Hello, Gordon Brown speaking . . . . Sorry about that little misunderstanding there with one of my team-mates . . . !' *(G.B.)*

In 1980 I was invited to take part in the Bob Hope Pro-Am golf tournament at Turnberry golf course in Ayrshire. There were many celebrities from the megastar world taking part and I was over the moon to have been invited. Being a member of Royal Troon and Old Prestwick golf clubs, I would not be overawed by Turnberry itself; but the large crowds and the television cameras – they were a totally different thing! On hearing of my invitation, I popped in to see my mum and dad at their house in Troon. Both my parents were delighted that I would be taking part. My mum asked me, 'What form does the tournament take?' I replied, 'It's a celebrity playing with three amateurs'. 'Super, and who's the celebrity *you* are playing with?' asked my mum. *(G.B.)*

In 1982 Gareth Edwards and I were golfing at Renfrew golf club just outside Glasgow in the Telly Savalas Pro-Am Golf. We were both standing on the first tee, which was surrounded by a very large crowd, practising our swings and trying our hardest to look like true golfers. Suddenly a lady rushed out of the crowd across the tee with an autograph book in her hand. She went straight past me to Gareth and said, 'Gareth, I'm a Scot and a rugby fanatic. Please let me have your autograph. You're the greatest rugby player that has ever played at Murrayfield. I always wished that you had been Scots.' Gareth of course was delighted and dutifully signed the autograph: *To Betty, with love and kisses, Gareth —* and he then turned round and gave me the autograph book and the pen. The lady looked at me aghast, totally ignorant of who I was – and, remember, she was a Scot *and* a rugby fanatic. I did not know whether to sign the book and hand it back to her to get the usual retort of 'Who's that?' or whether just to hand back the book to the lady unsigned. When, after possibly only five or six seconds, although it seemed like a lifetime, the lady's face broke in recognition and she said, 'You used to be Gordon Brown.' I duly signed the autograph *Gordon Brown* and, after it, *used to be.*   *(G.B.)*

In 1985 I took part in the Glasgow marathon. It was a magnificent experience and the cheering Glasgow crowds, who lined the whole route of the 26 plus miles, certainly brought a lump to my throat. Nearing the end of the marathon, I was getting very tired, and, having taken my last drink of water at the last watering hole, I set off on the final two miles. Just ahead was a small group of St John's Ambulance people attending to some of the wearied runners. As I gently made my way past them, a young blonde girl aged about eighteen called out to me, 'Would you like your legs rubbed, sir?' I replied 'No, thank you,' and went on my way. I had only gone about 20 yards past this lovely young lady when it dawned on me what I had just refused! But, despite my mind wanting me to stop and turn and go back to her, I couldn't get my body to obey, so I just went ever onwards. Eventually I reached the home straight at Glasgow Green, and, the further I ran up the straight the louder the crowd seemed to cheer. Inwardly I had a lovely feeling of pride and joy, thinking: they have recognized me. I was immediately brought back to earth. One of the disabled wheelchaired runners whizzed past me and sped on his way up the mall.   *(G.B.)*

6
THE BIGGEST BELL IN BUENOS AIRES

In Argentina during a Scottish tour five or six of us were making our way home from a cocktail party at the British embassy at around 2 a.m. when on impulse we decided to play 'Knock Down Ginger', where you ring the doorbell and run away. Childish of us, but we were well soused and it seemed like a good idea at the time. The giant second-row forward Peter Stagg, who stands 6 foot 10 in his stockinged feet, was not prepared to mess about ringing little doorbells, either. He would ring the biggest bell in Buenos Aires. So we roamed the streets looking for something sufficiently impressive, and at last he stepped up to the huge, imposing façade of the Bank of Argentina and plunged his finger on the buzzer. We waited, not expecting much of a response at this hour. Suddenly the bank doors rumbled open, and out stepped two armed security guards with sub-machine guns. So far as I can recall, none of us has played 'Knock Down Ginger' since. *(G.B.)*

On another of Scotland's tours of Argentina, Sandy Carmichael, the giant Scottish prop, was determined to capture as much of the tour on film as possible. He had taken with him a large cine camera, and everywhere we went in the country we heard its whirr. During one of the internal flights, from a town called Mar del Plata to Buenos Aires, Sandy decided to join the pilot in the cockpit because we were to fly at a fairly low altitude and the plane was a small Dakota. He had no sooner joined the pilot when the plane started to bob around. It had hit some pockets of air turbulence; each lasted only a few minutes, so we weren't too bothered to begin with. Unfortunately the dipping and weaving gradually got worse and worse, until eventually the plane was bouncing around like a ping-pong ball. We were growing very alarmed and the ground below seemed at times to be getting nearer and nearer. There was a middle-aged lady sitting beside me and she gradually became totally hysterical. I was spending more time attempting to reassure her than I was worrying about the movements of the plane. The air hostess tried to come and help me but because of the severity of the bobbing she was unable to walk up the aisle. The lady passenger then started screaming her head off. In an attempt to calm her, I grabbed both of her hands and clasped them tightly: she in return dug her teeth into the back of my hand. I started to scream beside her! I looked in despair at the air hostess and she motioned me to slap the woman in the face. I thought to myself: bloody hell, I don't even know the woman. However, there was nothing else for it: I was prepared to do anything to extract her teeth. Almost simultaneously with the slap, the plane bumped onto the runway at Buenos Aires airport and, as we gradually pulled to a stop, the lady slowly quietened and then started sobbing uncontrollably. She had drawn blood from my hand.

Eventually we found ourselves safe and sound inside the terminal building and all the boys were talking about what a terrible landing it had been. I said that really I hadn't noticed too much because of this damned woman who had been sitting beside me having hysterics. Big Sandy Carmichael, who I had totally forgotten had been in the cockpit throughout, immediately jumped up and shouted, 'Don't worry, Broonie, I've got every detail on film for you to see tonight!'   *(G.B.)*

On another occasion during a Scottish tour of Argentina, Ian Robertson, our stand-off, was very excited about one thing in particular. He could not wait to go to one of the grand ranches where some of the greatest thoroughbred racehorses are bred for distribution throughout the world. Robertson had regaled us with many stories about his horse-racing days and we all had the impression that he could have ridden any horse anywhere in the world. Eventually his dream came true and we went out to visit a ranch. No sooner had we seen one thoroughbred mating with a mare than a beautiful horse was brought out for us to have a look at. Robbo was ecstatic, swearing that it was one of the finest animals that he had ever cast his eyes on: 'This has to be a Derby winner in the making.' The owner of the ranch invited Robbo to ride it and his eyes stuck out like gobstoppers. 'Oh, please, could I?' he exclaimed. We applauded politely as the great equine expert mounted his steed. Then Ian McLauchlan, the prop-forward, slapped the animal good-naturedly on the backside. It galloped off, terrorized. Obviously Robbo was not in control. The horse sped off amongst some trees, and Robertson threw up his hands, grasping a low-hanging branch to save himself. As the horse galloped off into the sunset, it left Robbo dangling pathetically from the branch, like the Range Rider. Sandy Carmichael sprinted to the tree to take Robbo's picture. The photo turned out rather well – except that the subject had refused to smile. *(G.B.)*

In Argentina one year I was walking down a street in Buenos Aires with several team-mates when all of a sudden hysterical screaming broke out from about one hundred yards away. The next thing we heard was the crack of gunfire. We were aware of people sprinting hell for leather towards us, obviously terror-stricken. We then realized that the guy firing the gun was coming behind them, which meant that he was coming *towards us*! I immediately dived into a doorway, knocking down two people in the process and landing on top of one of them. As the bullets from this maniac's gun splattered the walls round about us the gentleman lying under me evidently recognizing some of my expletives, asked, 'Are you one of the Scottish rugby players?' As I tried to get my head lower in the doorway, I replied, 'Yes, my name is Gordon Brown.' His answer stunned me 'My God,' he said, 'I am from Troon too! Would you believe it?' I replied that at that particular moment I was prepared to believe *anything*. 'Och, don't worry, this is a regular occurrence in this city. Tell me' he continued, as the bullets bounced off the nearby walls, 'has Joe Wilson still got the newsagent's shop in Troon?' *(G.B.)*

7

FOUL FETTLE IN FIJI

On our way home from a British Lions tour of New Zealand we stopped off in Fiji to play against the national team. The game was a fiasco. Here we were relaxing and enjoying ourselves at last with no pressure from statistics, press, public, telephone calls or the blooming rain. We were stiff, sore and tired after New Zealand and the last thing any of us wanted was to play against big, strong, fast and elusive Fijians on a pitch like concrete. Only half of our touring party were available for selection, so numerous were the injuries that we were carrying. Those of us who could just about play started hunting through our kitbags for jerseys, shorts and socks to wear. We turned out in a dreadful state: shorts which were anything but white, jerseys which were mainly burst and grubby, socks faded and full of holes. As both teams lined up to be introduced to the Governor General of Fiji, the comparison was embarrassing. The Fijians looked immaculate. Pure-white jerseys, jet-black shorts, black and white socks. Every one of them stood proudly erect showing off a mass of rippling muscles, like Olympic athletes, and with just a hint of expectant perspiration gleaming on their brows. We stood like half-shut knives, bleary-eyed, disorderly and uninterested. If a complete stranger had walked into the arena to be told that one of the world's top sides was to play the locals, there is no way he would have guessed which was which correctly.

The whole island seemed to be crammed in and around the small stadium. All the surrounding palm trees were teeming with human bodies, hanging on like grim death to every possible branch. When the Fijians scored a try early in the game, not only did the crowd in the stadium erupt but everybody fell out of the trees! The referee was such a joke that even we had to laugh. Somehow he seemed totally in character with the occasion. A penalty count against us of 23–2 summed up his view of the game perfectly.

Late in the second half I had to substitute for Trevor Evans, the Welsh wing-forward. I had always fancied a game in the back row but this was hardly the one I would have chosen. When Trevor limped off, I was sitting on the substitutes' bench at halfway, with my Achilles tendon throbbing painfully, and Fiji had just scored their second-last try. The conversion attempt was held up to allow me to take the field at this glorious moment in the proceedings. As I crossed the 25-yard line, one of my team-mates, standing behind the goal posts, yelled out, 'Forget it, Broonie! We'll do better without you!' This was the sight that met his eyes. I had on a pair of 32-inch shorts which were so tight that they restricted breathing, never mind tucking your jersey in. The jersey, on the other hand, looked like a teepee; torn and filthy, it dangled round my thighs so that my tiny shorts were completely obscured from view. The constriction of the shorts, and the agony of my Achilles tendon, meant that I had to shamble and limp the first 20 yards before I could get going, and as I watched my feet stumbling over the 25-yard line, I noticed a final touch of class setting off the whole outfit – my own everyday ankle socks.   *(G.B.)*

Although our stay in Fiji lasted only three days, it certainly had a strong effect on all of us and helped in some way to heal many of the wounds which had been opened during the tour of New Zealand. On the second day, we were lying beside the swimming pool at our hotel; the sun was beating down, the beer was flowing freely, and we were all very happy. A thought crossed Fran Cotton's mind. Not, you may say, a particularly long or adventurous journey; the primadonnas among the backs reckon the forwards in every team all share one brain between them – in fact, we do occasionally have our moments. 'You know, boys,' Cotton mused, 'the Four Home Unions Committee have got it the wrong way round – we should spend three months in Fiji and four days in New Zealand.' There was not one dissenting voice.   *(B.W.)*

One of the many attractions of Fiji is the Pacific Harbour golf course. Before leaving I had time for a round there with Mike Gibson, John Bevan and Allan Lewis. On the first tee John Bevan had a big practice swing and the golf club flew out of his grasp into the nearby jungle, never to be found again. He then hit his ball up the middle of the fairway, only to hook it with his second strike right into the jungle. So, after only two blows, he was already down one club and one ball. He shrugged his shoulders. 'Things can only improve.' he said philosophically. 'Yes,' Allan Lewis reassured him, 'you've got thirteen clubs and eight balls still to go!' Halfway round the course I crashed the two-seater buggy which Mike Gibson and I were travelling in. As it tipped over, I was thrown clear but Mike was jammed underneath it as it careered downhill at a crazy angle. After a worrying interval, Mike hauled himself clear. 'Dear God,' he said as he struggled back up the hill, 'after all I've been through in New Zealand' (the poor devil had been dogged by unrelenting bad luck throughout our tour), 'at least let me survive a round of *golf* in Fiji!'

(G.B.)

8

A CHEEKY GRIN

On the British Lions tour of South Africa one of the matches was against a Border XV in the town of East London. The game was a pretty boring affair and certainly no contest for the Lions. The only memorable moment involved Mike Burton, the English prop-forward. Mike had his shorts torn off him and had to get a new pair to replace them. He ran from the far side of the pitch across to the main stand, where the British Lions baggage man was, and eventually a new pair of shorts was produced. Now Mike, being very large, found it difficult to get a pair of shorts which fitted him; the only pair he managed to get on were so tight that he could not tuck his Lion's jersey under them – the Lion's jerseys were so long that it looked as if Mike had no shorts on at all. He turned to run across the pitch to rejoin play with his jersey flapping around his thighs and as he got to the halfway line he stopped, turned and looked back at the stand with a mischievous expression. Then he very slowly grabbed the tail of his shirt and flipped it up, revealing a bare backside. His shorts had obviously not covered it properly. He gave us two or three wiggles in the stand and then he squeezed his shorts up over his bottom and ran across to join the match. The whole stand was in uproar. The British Lions tour manager, Alan Thomas, had a very red face, but hoped the game could now proceed without any further embarrassment. Fate was unkind. Ten minutes later (with the game *barely* underway again) Mike Burton was once more separated from his breeches, and ran over to the main stand to rummage in the baggage for replacements. The game was again held up as he poured himself, grunting, into yet another pair of shorts several sizes too small, with his Lion's jersey dangling down outside. As he turned to run across the pitch, the entire stand buzzed expectantly. Burton, not without a sense of occasion, ran to the halfway line, stopped, looked over his shoulder at the main stand, and ceremoniously clasped the hem of his Lions jersey. There was a gasp – then a groan of disappointment – as the Burton backside was disclosed, discreetly covered by Burton's shorts. The owner turned towards us and wagged a finger censoriously, giving a little – cheeky – grin.   *(B.W.)*

The Scottish Rugby Union has been renowned over the years for stinginess but the best story to illustrate the way things used to be revolves round the late great Jock Wemyss, one of Scotland's greatest forwards. Jock received his first caps just before the Second World War and was the only capped player to be selected for the first international following the war. As the secretary of the Scottish Rugby Union was handing out the international jerseys prior to the kick-off, he walked past Jock, totally ignoring him. Jock was taken aback by this and said to the secretary, 'What about my jersey?' The secretary replied, 'You've already got one.'
(B.W.)

When I played for Scotland we were given one rugby jersey per season. If at the end of an international you swapped that jersey and were subsequently selected again you had to pay 11 guineas for a new one. We also in those days had to produce our own shorts and our own navy blue socks. The giant second-row forward Peter Stagg turned up to play one international at Murrayfield with two huge holes in his socks. I said to him, 'You're not going on the field with these two great holes, are you?' 'Of course not', he said, 'don't worry!' He then proceeded to take out black boot polish and blacken his legs where the holes were. I had to admit it was quite effective.   *(G.B.)*

I once played for Marr rugby club against Irvine when the Marr hooker was having a terrible time seeing the ball as the Marr scrum-half tried to put it into the scrum. The hooker's problem was that the Irvine tighthead's hair was so long that it hung right down over the mouth of the tunnel. The Marr hooker eventually complained bitterly to the referee, who reckoned that the complaint was quite justified. He turned to the Irvine tighthead prop and said to him, 'Go and get your hair tied back.' The whole game was held up while the prop went off. Eventually he came back on to the field. I will never forget the sight. Unable to find any elastoplast or scrumcap, he had been forced to tie back his hair with – a blue ribbon. I think his Irvine team-mates still pull his leg about it to this day. *(G.B.)*

9

A PIG IN THE BUSH

On tour with the Welsh team in Australia, we were playing in the outback at a place called Cobar. The day before the game, six of us fixed up to go on a wild pig shoot. We left the hotel at six in the morning crammed into a small jeep, each of us loaded down with belts of ammunition, double-barrelled and pump-action shotguns. We all looked like a bunch of hill-billies. We travelled around the bush for twelve to fourteen hours in temperatures of over 100°. During this time we never fired one shot. We did see a pig, but the driver got so excited he ran the poor bastard over. *(B.W.)*

Tourists sometimes come to our shores and in 1968 it was the turn of the Australians. In the traditional opening fixture of touring sides, Australia played Oxford University. Ollie Waldron, the Irish prop, was then playing with the university. The Australians were endeavouring to impose themselves on the university side; especially in the scrum. In the first incident of the game, the Australian hooker, Ross Cullen, bit deeply into the unprotected Ollie Waldron's ear. Cullen was dismissed by the referee, but the referee's judgement did little for Waldron's drooping ear. In the dressing room after the game Waldron was trying desperately to take off his jersey without pulling his torn ear with it. One of his team-mates came over to him and put his arm around him and said 'Waldron, you are now Eton and Oxford.'

Waldron was not the only Irish prop-forward to provoke humour in the

'. . . six of us fixed up to go on a wild pig shoot.'

scrum. In the early seventies Phil O'Callaghan was penalized by the referee Merion Joseph for an infringement in the scrum. Joseph signalled a penalty against O'Callaghan, stating that he was 'boring'. O'Callaghan quickly retorted, 'You are not too entertaining yourself, ref.'   *(F.S.)*

When Scotland toured Australia a while ago, one day after training we went down to the beach called Surfer's Paradise, just outside Brisbane. We were lying back in the brilliant sunshine, listening to the waves rolling in and the distant sound of a seagull. We were enjoying the odd can of lager and the sight of the odd girl walking up and down the beach in a brief bikini. Suddenly Billy Steele, the Scotland and Langholm wing, said out loud to nobody in particular, 'Hey, boys, do you know that today is the Langholm Common Riding?' referring of course to the annual festival held in the small town of Langholm in the Scottish Borders. We totally ignored him. The response he got was absolutely nil. After a few moments he looked up to the bright blue skies and exclaimed, 'Hey, they've got a great day for it.'   *(G.B.)*

In 1976 England played Australia in Brisbane. That game has become renowned for a colossal and horrendous punch-up which commenced immediately after the kick-off. Before the teams could settle down, Mike Burton was penalized and ordered off for a late tackle. The Australian full-back had fielded a high up and under and following his catch he kicked the ball into touch. He no sooner had kicked the ball when Burton tackled him – a move adjudged to be late by the referee. Burton to this day claims that it could not have been that late because, after all, he did get there as soon as he could.   *(B.W.)*

10

'I'M GOING TO EAT HIM'

The one-time Welsh loosehead forward John Lloyd was renowned for eating any sort and any amount of food which came his way. In one of his momentous team talks, Clive Rowland had built the Welsh side up to a crescendo ten minutes before kick-off. He had slowly gone through the whole team exhorting each man to greater things. Finally he turned to John Lloyd and screamed, 'And you, Lloyd, what are you going to do to your opposite number?' John Lloyd's eyes flickered for a moment as he digested this important question. 'I'm going to eat him!' he bellowed. End of team talk. *(B.W.)*

When I was playing for Wales against France in 1975, at the first scrum and every scrum after that in the first half, the French 2nd row Esteve was punching me through the scrum. At half-time, I told Charlie and Pricey that I'd had enough and that at the first scrum in the second half I was going to 'boot him' in the 'chops'. I was as good as my word and a fight erupted. The referee was blowing his whistle and after many blasts the fighting ceased, but a French forward was seen to throw the last punch. The referee awarded Wales a penalty. I watched Esteve walking back. He looked over his shoulder at me – and winked. I turned to Charlie and said, 'What shall I do now? The bastard's going to kill me.' Charlie looked at me and said, 'Try telling him he's wanted on the phone.'

(B.W.)

The greatest scrum-half that the world has ever seen is none other than Wales's Gareth Edwards. Gareth is king of rugby in his home country and is revered like royalty everywhere he goes. Recently Gareth was suffering terribly from constipation and went to see his doctor. Following an examination by the doctor, who was one of Gareth's greatest fans, he was told he would need to take some medicine. The doctor duly prepared a prescription. On the prescription he wrote *Ambre Solaire Suppositories*. The diagnosis was that the sun shone out of Gareth's backside.

(B.W.)

Gareth Edwards is a great friend of mine and when we are away on long tours with the British Lions we golf regularly together. However, he once smashed me on the nose with a tremendous punch during an international at Murrayfield between Scotland and Wales. He had been stamped on in the middle of a ruck by one of my team-mates. He was jumping about like a dervish, screaming oaths galore in Scotland's direction. I was just getting up from the ruck and was on one knee when he thumped me. He ran off down the pitch to follow the play, with me after him shouting, 'What the hell was that for, ya wee bugger?' My nose was very sore! The Welsh number 8, Mervyn Davies, grabbed me, fearing that I was going to administer retribution, but he immediately realized from the look on my face that that was the furthest thing from my mind. I shouted to Gareth to keep out of my way for the remainder of the game but he knew I was only bluffing. After the match he apologized for the punch and we both had a good laugh about it. Mind you, my nose was still guy stingy! 'Well, Broonie,' he said with a glint in his eye, 'that will make up for all the times that I have wanted to punch you during tours, for keeping me awake at night with your bloody awful snoring!'

(G.B.)

All players selected for Wales had to undergo a medical with the WRU doctor. If you failed the medical, you would have to drop out of the team. We were waiting to go in for examination and Charlie Faulkner was getting worried about answering the questions correctly. I was in first and had the medical. The first question I was asked was: if I had my left eye covered up, what would I be? I replied, 'Partly blind, sir.' The second question was: if I had my right eye covered up as well, what would I be? I replied, 'Totally blind, sir.' The doctor said, 'That is correct. On your way out, send the next one in.' On seeing Charlie, who was next in, I said, 'Don't worry, it's easy. The answers are: partially blind and totally blind.'

Charlie sat down and had his medical, then the doctor asked him the first question. 'If I cut off your left ear, what would you be?' Charlie replied, 'Partially blind, sir.' Second question: 'If I then cut off your right ear, what would you be?' Charlie replied, 'Totally blind, sir.' The astonished doctor then said, 'Charlie, how the hell do you make that out?' Charlie answered, 'Well, my hat would fall over my eyes!'   *(B.W.)*

A Welsh Valleys rugby club on tour in America was staying in a huge hotel in San Francisco. On coming back from a night out, which included a very heavy drinking session, two of the players could not find their rooms. They decided to sleep in the corridor and so slid down on the floor ready to sleep. One of them heard talking coming from a room nearby. Thinking it might be some of their team-mates, they decided to look through the keyhole. What they saw astounded them. There in the room was a beautiful naked woman with a voluptuous figure. Standing by her was a man who was saying, 'Your face is so beautiful that I'm going to have it painted in gold. Your breasts are so magnificent that I'm going to have them painted in silver. Your thighs are so superb (for lack of a better word) that I'm going to have them painted in platinum.' During this time, the two boys outside the door were getting excited and jostling each other for the right of the keyhole. The man in the room, on hearing the noise at the door, turned and yelled, 'Who the hell is out there?' The two boys replied, 'We're two painters from Pontypool.'   *(B.W.)*

Before a Scotland–Wales international at Murrayfield, Gareth Edwards was walking along Princes Street having a breath of fresh air with one or two of the Welsh players. While he was standing looking in some shop windows, two or three Welsh supporters sidled up beside him. As they were rather shy they did not want immediately to engage Gareth in conversation, and catching this out the corner of his eye Gareth noticed that two were pushing the third forward. Eventually this one plucked up the courage to say something to Gareth and out came the immortal words! 'Up for the game then, Gar?'   *(B.W.)*

On tour with the Welsh team, John Dawes, the Welsh coach, informed the players that no long-distance phone calls would be paid for by the

WRU. The players knew that John Dawes was getting free phone calls. So one night, after a game and quite a few beers, Charlie said to me, 'Come on, Bob, let's go up and phone home.' When we got upstairs at the hotel, Charlie took me into John Dawes's room and said, 'Watch the door, we'll put this on John Dawes's bill.' He then rang the operator, gave her the number of his home and then gave her John Dawes's name and room number. The operator took the information and said she would ring back when she'd made the connection. After a minute or two the phone rang. Charlie picked it up and the operator said, 'Long-distance phone call for Mr John Dawes.' To which Charlie replied, 'I'm sorry he's not here,' and put the phone down.   *(B.W.)*

One of the highlights of any rugby player's career is to play on the Barbarians Easter tour of Wales. One of the fun highlights of the weekend is the golf match on the Sunday when every single player in the team has to take part whether or not he has held a golf club before. The competition is decided on a knock-out basis: some feel that the idea is to be knocked out as soon as possible, so that you can adjourn to the bar and enjoy the delights of the golf club.

In 1972 I took part in this tour and my team and I were duly knocked out early in the day. In my team was none other than Moss Keane, the Irish second-row forward. Being a typical Irishman, Moss's favourite drink was Guinness. He downed two pints of Guinness to every one pint of beer that I and my team-mates enjoyed.

When the golf tournament was over and the prizes had been presented, the Barbarians Vice President, Herbert Waddell, came over to me and said, 'Right, Bobby, you will need to get the boys on the bus so we can get back to the hotel for dinner.' I said, 'Let's have one more round of drinks and then we will set off.' He agreed. I then turned to my team-mates and said, 'OK, boys, one more drink all round.' By this time we had consumed about ten pints of beer – and Mossy at least twenty pints of Guinness. However, following my invitation for one more round, he sat shaking his head. I asked, 'Mossy, what's wrong with you? Don't you want another drink?' He looked up at me and with a twinkle in his eye he said, 'No, I don't, Bobby. To be sure, I don't want to be making a pig of myself.'   *(B.W.)*

On my selection for the Welsh team in 1973, I was informed that, for the after-match dinner, dinner suits had to be worn. At this time I was working short-time. I went to the secretary of the WRU and asked if there was any chance of a loan or some help to buy some evening shoes, because the sole of one of my shoes was hanging off. I was told to call at the WRU office later in the week. I purposely wore the shoes with the sole hanging off to back up my claim. On seeing the shoes, the secretary of the WRU put his hand in his pocket and pulled out a roll of £5, £10 and £20 notes with an elastic band wrapped around them. He took off the elastic band, threw it across the desk and said, 'This should help till your next pay day.' *(B.W.)*

Some time ago I journeyed down to South Wales to a town called Peny-craig to play for a Carwyn James XV against a Welsh Valleys XV. The match was to help celebrate Welsh Valleys Year. It was indeed a great honour to be asked by Carwyn, and his international team read like a Who's Who of British rugby superstars. Gareth Edwards, David Duckham, Gerald Davies – to name but a few. A crowd of at least 30,000 was packed into this ground and HTV's cameras were there to record all the excitement. At the first line-out I looked at my opposite number: he must have been about 5 foot 9. As the ball was thrown into the line-out and I jumped to catch it, this wee fellow punched me. This was repeated in the next four line-outs and eventually I said to the referee, 'For God's sake, referee, I haven't driven all the way down from Scotland to take part in this match just to have the crap punched out of me. Nor have I come down here to punch some wee Welsh guy.' The referee's reply was, 'Come on Broonie, you can sort it out for yourself.' In the next line-out I only half jumped, and at the same time I smacked this wee guy right in the mush. He stood there smiling at me and said, through his grin, 'I wondered how long it would take you,' He never came near me again for the rest of the night! *(G.B.)*

11

ENGLAND, THEIR ENGLAND

I like reading stuff that confirms my own well-developed prejudices. I like seeing the mighty fall. I like seeing well-known sporting names hitting a period of banana skinitis. 'Cop a load of that, smartie pants.'

This happens in spades when you've been dropped and you're sitting on the replacements' bench. I can remember being in such a position at Twickenham watching England against Ireland, sitting wrapped in my England tracksuit enveloped by an old woollen blanket to keep out the February chills and muttering things like 'Come on, you green machine'.

Yet I'm not even consistent. When I was definitely in the 2nd XV Wednesday, dirttrackers, driftwood, etc., etc., team on the British Lions tour in 1974. I could sit on the replacement bench on a Saturday and cheer for the first team and really want them to win.

I have never been able to explain this. However, as Bobby Windsor keeps telling me, 'Andy, you've always been a pillock.' (A.R.)

Before a Scotland–England game at Twickenham the Scottish rugby team visited a theatre in London which was showing *Pyjama Tops*. We were delighted to be going to this play because it featured none other than Fiona Richmond, the young lady from *Men Only* magazine whose sexual exploits were put down in print each month. She and numerous others paraded about on stage that night in various stages of undress. In the middle of the stage there was a huge glass-sided swimming pool and various of the young ladies swam nude in this during the course of the

'. . . clad in only a Scottish rugby jersey.'

play, the plot of which was rather thin, although that did not bother us one little bit. Following Miss Richmond's swim in the pool she climbed out and quickly towelled herself down, swaying the towel round her head and throwing it into the audience. It hit my brother, Peter, right between the eyes, much to the hilarity of the rest of the team. Undaunted, Peter stood up, rolled the towel back into a ball and hurled it back onto the stage, hitting Miss Richmond right between the eyes in turn. It brought the house down. The finale to the whole show was when Miss Richmond appeared from the depths of the swimming pool clad in only a Scottish rugby jersey. The donor has yet to be identified.   *(G.B.)*

One year Scotland played against England at Twickenham. The game was a ding-dong battle from start to finish and I was up against Nigel Horton, the England second-row forward, who was well known for his very physical way of playing the game. I got the better of Nigel in a ruck just before full-time. When the full-time whistle blew, heralding Scotland's victory by 16 points to 15, I sought out all the England players to shake their hands. When I approached Nigel he punched away my hand, proclaiming, 'Brown, next Saturday I'm going to bloody well kill you.' He was referring to the match between Scotland and England the following Saturday at Murrayfield to celebrate one hundred years of the fixture between the two countries. To this day I am eternally grateful to the English rugby selectors for apparently saving my life. They dropped big Nigel from the game.   *(G.B.)*

When the England and British Lions hooker Peter Wheeler brought out his autobiography he was signing copies of it in a large departmental store in London. Quite a queue formed. One young lady stepped forward and thrust the book under Peter's nose. He looked up at her and said, 'How do you wish it endorsed?' She smiled a beautiful smile, looked him straight in the eye and said, 'Just sign it *From one hooker to another.*'
                    (B.W.)

England were playing Australia at Twickenham in a game not remembered for much except for what happened at half-time – when a young lady called Erica Rowe decided to run across the pitch and surprise everyone and delight most. Bill Beaumont, the England captain who has the biggest backside in international rugby, was busy cajoling his players on to better efforts in the second half. Standing with his back to Erica, he was unaware of what was happening, but as he looked at his players he realized that he did not have their full attention. He shouted at them, 'Boys, Boys, what is it? You're not paying attention to me.' Steve Smith, the English scrum-half, said, 'Well, Bill, there's a guy has just run on the park with your backside on his chest.' *(F.S.)*

One million eyes moved by British Rail (Southern
  Region) every day.
Two belong to me, although they have increasingly less
  to say.

A pillar of society, a veritable cog in Maggie Thatcher's
  grand plan.
I'm the definitive 7.59 East Grinstead to Cannon Street
  Station, English commuter man.

Oh once I had Pacific ambition and coral hopes and far
  away dreams.
But only just last week I got seduced, by a non-
  contributory index-linked company pension scheme.

But if you cut the surface of my hopes and then continue
  to scratch,
You'll find I've got a ticket for a Scotland *v.* England
  Rugby Football Match.

Now, I know the Scots loathe and hate us Sassenachs,
  both on and off the Isle of Skye.
But quite frankly from my privileged position in the
  Home Counties I've never, really, fully understood
  why.

Now, I mean, against Culloden, Butcher Cumberland and
  the slaughter at Glencoe.
We English have had to put up with Moira Anderson,
  Andy Stewart, the Bay City Rollers and even Edgar
  Allen Poe.

However now I too know that life is an English-inspired
   anti-Scottish conspiracy.
Since in the World Cup we were in easy Group One and
   the Scottish stuffed into impossible Group Three:

Still who cares, next Saturday it's the Calcutta Cup
   Match and we can open old wounds again.
At Twickenham, as fifteen nasty Scotsmen line up against
   fifteen fabulous Englishmen.

The final result?
Well really I don't mind one way or the other.
– Because I might be an English Commuter Man, but I
   had a Scottish Grandmother   *(A.R.)*

Sometimes, but increasingly less frequently, I get invited to send a contribution to a rugby tour magazine. This is one I sent to a pal, Keith
Richardson, for the Wycliffe College Tour to Canada Magazine. Keith
used to play prop for Gloucester. He hasn't spoken to me since I sent this
contribution as he thought it was silly. He was not wrong.

SPACE-FILLER (INTER-GALACTIC)

Slowly but surely the fourth Baron de Wycliffe inched his way along the
icy ledge. The wind howled out an old Elvis number – 'Are you lonesome
tonight'. He was.

   The Baron, a closet cross-dresser, had once been a fourth-rate table
dancer in Young Street, Toronto. But fate had dealt him an unkind blow.
He was surplus to requirements and had fallen in with the evil and fat
Keith Richardson. The Baron's feeble mind recollected in the original
Gothic script a poem by Goethe and at the same time remembered how
the mind-chillingly devious Keith Richardson used to drop the 'on' from
his name and pretend to be a former rock 'n' roller, simply to impress
his mum.

   Suddenly the wind reached a crescendo of total boredom and with a
lack of expectation the Baron was ripped untimely from his mother's
womb. Tomorrow and tomorrow and tomorrow. When he had grown up

he'd always wanted to be a plant. Now that would be impossible. Keith Richardson has a lot to answer for.

Especially getting his friends to write stuff for the 'fabulous-Wycliffe-College-fabulous-Tour-to-Canada-Magazine!!'

Here's a tip, kids – don't buy this magazine, it may damage your wallet; and secondly don't die on tour. It's very inconvenient.

> Lots of Love 'n' Fabness
> *Andy Ripley*

P.S. Be smart – get a good job in a bank.   *(A.R.)*

Wise owls may hint at the fact that you should grow old with grace. The silly response is: show me grace and I'll grow old with her. The even sillier response is: no, why should I?

Talking about silly questions and responses. . . . It is March 1986. Having just been in the Middlesex team which won the county championship, I get a phone call from Twickenham. It's Don Rutherford, who says, 'How would you like to play in the England seven-a-side team in Australia next month?'

Eleven years after my last appearance, aged thirty-eight, my England recall. Quick as a flash I respond. 'You're not Don Rutherford at all. You're the nutcase who's been phoning up players on the fringe of the England squad and telling them they've been selected.'

'No. I am Don Rutherford. Yes, I am a nutcase. However, due to circumstances beyond my control, it looks like it's a choice between you and a hatstand. Quite frankly, between you and me, the hatstand got quite a few votes.'

So there I was, on the plane out to Australia . . . Oh yes, Nigel Melville was injured, so I was also now captain of the side. Well, we didn't actually play brilliantly but we had a good time; the high spot was at Bahrain airport on the way home at 1.00 in the morning, reading the John Reason report in the *Sunday Telegraph*. Huw Thomas, the Sale winger, was so inspired that he wrote the following poem on the plane in about half an hour.

THE NEW SOUTH WALES SEVENS

(On first reading Reason's Telegraph)

This is an ode to mark England's demise,
A team that sent out to a Spanish surprise.
That team we played, and we had to defeat
But we took no account of the intense Sydney heat.

The group we were in, at first glance, seemed quite good,
As number two seeds of the four we had stood,
Favoured to go through to the final day's play,
But we failed to subdue the 'Spanish Olé'!

Australia, we knew, were a strong proposition,
With the other two teams offering scant opposition.
But the Spanish team – well, they'd other plans,
To the increasing delight of the New South Wales fans.

Soon the opening two matches had already passed
And we were in danger of finishing last,
With a play-off 'gainst a Dutch team to us unknown
Whose confidence by now must surely have grown.

Despite out-of-depth Bond, and Rippers and Pete
Our team were quite sure that the Dutch they could beat
But some 'experts' felt that the team lacked ideas
And it seemed that the Dutch would confirm their worst
    fears.

With full-time approaching, the Dutch were ahead
And many a man could with justice have said,
'England can't tackle, can't pass and are slow!'
But we still had some time left to finish the show.

With two minutes left, Fran Clough made a score,
And Richard Hill's kick gave us two points more.
There were still forty seconds, 'Could the Pomms win?'
No! Everyone thought that our chances were slim.

The Dutch kicked the ball off to restart the game.
The ball stayed in play – it was really quite tame.

If that had been Williams, it would surely have gone out
And the Dutch would be in with a definite shout.

Instead, for a change, the ball went to Winters,
Who handles the ball as if made of splinters.
On then to Williams, so lethargic and slow,
Who passed it to Bondie and he couldn't go.

On the opposite side to Rippers the Banker
Was a man still chasing the invisible flanker.
He ran to the try-line and over it dived.
Then two seconds later full-time had arrived.

England at last had defeated a team,
Despite trying hard to lose, it would seem.
The team then were happy, at least for a bit –
The next day, on the hill, in the sun, they could sit.

So then, on the Sunday the sun's rays did reach
The players from England, all strewn on the beach.
No longer concerned at the jeers of the fans,
The lads had their minds on the growth of their tans.

So with vengeance the flight home it came,
With a brief look at the 'Sundays' in downtown Bahrain.
'There is the *Telegraph*. Let's read old John Reason.'
And that was the highlight of our '86 season!!

An account to tarnish some budding careers,
Or quickly dismiss the last fifteen years
Of players who'd given much time to the game
And now were the scum of the earth to a name.

This then, the result of a long trip to see
The New South Wales Sevens, and all of it free.
The press had come up with some arguments flimsy,
Slagging the boys off, all except Simmsy!

So we come back to England, there to get stick,
This was the Seven that the Spanish could lick.
But the lads have had fun, all to a man,
Happy to know that they'd got the best tan!

The plane touched down at Heathrow. From being captain of the England VII, two weeks later I just managed to make the bench for the Rosslyn Park 2nd VII in the Middlesex Sevens. Oh, the crests and troughs of life.

(A.R.)

12

AFRICAN AFFLICTION

Mike Burton, the English prop-forward, was renowned for being a real character on all the tours he went on. One day when he and I were walking down the street in Cape Town, South Africa, during the British Lions tour, he said to me, 'Bobby, you don't do very well with the girls. Why don't you stick around with me and maybe you would learn a thing or two.' As we walked down the street he spied two girls standing on a street corner having a chat with each other. He immediately turned to me and said, 'Bobby, come with me and listen to some decent patter.' He swaggered over to the two girls. Unbeknown to him, both were young ladies of ill-repute. He said to the one on the left, 'Come on, darling, I'm Mickey Burton from Gloucester and I can give you something that you have never had.' She turned to her companion and said, 'Elizabeth, here's one with leprosy.' *(B.W.)*

In South Africa, Bobby Windsor, the Welsh hooker, was very adept at making all his phone calls home to his wife from the manager's room. This was saving Bobby a lot of money because the manager's bill was being paid by the four Home Unions Tour Committee. However, the team manager realized something was wrong, as he was getting huge accounts to settle when he was only making one or two calls himself. He therefore instructed the hotel to make a note of all numbers being dialled to Britain. As we were leaving one hotel, the manager was asked to pay for an account that he was certain was not his. When he had inquired about the numbers dialled, he came onto the team bus and shouted, 'Someone has been using my phone and not paying the bill. If the culprit doesn't

own up now, there is going to be trouble.' Total silence reigned, though of course we knew whom he was referring to. He eventually stood up and said, 'OK. The culprit can now be found out. The number that was dialled was Newport 2379.' As quick as a flash Bobby Windsor jumped to his feet and shouted up the bus, 'Which one of you bastards has been phoning my wife?' *(F.S.)*

We were beating every team we met in South Africa, though we were always told by someone, 'Wait till you play so-and-so. They'll kick the shit out of you guys.' Everywhere that Ian McLauchlan, the Mighty Mouse prop, went people kept saying to him, 'Wait till you go to Transvaal and play against Johann Strauss. He is the biggest and best prop in the world and he will murder you.' The week before we played the Transvaal we had a game against a select XV, like a Barbarians team representing South Africa. Picked to play tight-head prop for this select XV was the one and only Johann Strauss. That day, however, Ian McLauchlan was not playing for the Lions; instead it was Mike Burton, the English loose-head prop. Just before we took the field, Mike said to me, 'Broonie, I want all the help you can give me today in the scrums against this big fellow Strauss, because if I do well today against him, who knows, maybe next Saturday I'll be selected for the Lions to play Transvaal rather than the Mighty Mouse.' Not long after the game kicked off a scrum was called. As it formed up, I looked at Johann Strauss for the first time in my life and I could not believe it – he was absolutely colossal. The thought went through my mind: Mickey, this guy is going to murder you. We formed up about ten yards apart and clattered down together; no sooner had the front rows met than I heard Mickey Burton say, 'Hello, Johann, I'm Mickey Burton from Gloucester.' Smack!!! Mickey punched him right on the nose. My immediate reaction was: God! Mickey, what have you done? He's going to kill you. However, no sooner had the two front rows come together again at the second scrum than I heard Mickey Burton say, 'Hello, Johann, remember me? Mickey Burton from Gloucester.' Smack!!! Mickey had punched him on the nose once again. I thought: Mickey, you've just started what must be the Third World War. Five minutes later we formed up for the next scrum and Johann Strauss was

'Bobby Windsor was very adept at making all his phone calls home to his wife from the manager's office.'

shaking his head looking straight at Mickey Burton and saying to him, 'Don't punch me again. I don't like it.' He came into the scrum as quiet as a wee lamb. Mickey then proceeded to turn him inside out in the scrummages for the rest of the match.

The following Saturday the two teams were announced. Ian McLauchlan was propping for the British Lions but there was no Johann Strauss in the Transvaal team. The selectors had felt that, if he could not handle Mike Burton, the second-choice loose-head prop, how on earth could he handle the mighty Ian McLauchlan? *(G.B.)*

During a British Lions tour of South Africa Gareth Edwards, the Welsh scrum-half, and Roger Young, the Irish scrum-half, became inseparable friends. They went everywhere together, golfing, swimming, fishing, etc., and by the time they left South Africa to come home their friendship had been sealed for life. The following international rugby season saw Ireland visiting Cardiff and the Welsh coach, Clive Rowlands, left Gareth Edwards in no doubt what he was to do to Roger Young that day, irrespective of their superb friendship. Fired by his coach's exhortations, Gareth took the field prepared to do battle with Roger. The game had no sooner kicked off than the referee called for a scrum down. As Gareth approached the scrum to put the ball in, Roger Young turned to him, tapped him on the shoulder and said, 'Hey, Gar, you didn't answer my last letter.' *(B.W.)*

It was the first Test against South Africa, and I ran out onto the pitch with the rest of the team in front of a 70,000 crowd who were booing and jeering. The British Lions team huddled together near the halfway line waiting for the Springboks team to appear. When they did, they came out of the tunnel so fast that one of the British Lions' players said, 'Jesus Christ, we must be on the wrong pitch.' The last member of the South African team to emerge from the tunnel was a 6 foot 6, 18-stone, one-eyed flanker. We had heard rumours that this player had a killing instinct (we had nicknamed him Cyclops for obvious reasons). Gareth Edwards turned to us and said, 'Bloody hell, the rest of the team must be running away from him.' *(B.W.)*

'Bloody hell, the rest of the team must be running away from him.'

On the flight to South Africa one year I was taken ill with food poisoning. I was so bad they took me to the back of the plane, where a nurse told me to suck ice-cubes to cool me down. Not knowing this, Ken Kennedy, the team doctor, came to the back of the plane and put a thermometer under my tongue. On taking it out of my mouth, he said, 'Well, looking at this, Bobby died twenty-four hours ago.'   *(B.W.)*

Some of our scrummage practice sessions in South Africa were very tough – in fact, far tougher than what we encountered during the games. In one of these sessions the scrums collapsed and a scream came from the opposition pack. We quickly broke up and found Chris Ralston, the English second-row forward, lying in a crumpled heap on the ground clutching his shoulder. Bobby Windsor quietly bent down on one knee. 'What is it, Chris?' he asked anxiously. 'What have you done?' 'It's my bloody shoulder,' said Ralston. 'Is it sore?' asked Bobby. 'It's *excruciating!*' replied Ralston, his face creased with pain. 'Yes,' said Bobby, 'but is it sore?'   *(F.S.)*

We were coming into land at Cape Town airport and the pilot had just finished telling us about our time of arrival, etc., when over the intercom, unknown to the pilot, came his voice as he spoke to the co-pilot. 'As soon as we get down I'm going to have a bath, I'm going to have a drink and then I'm going to make love to that beautiful, big, blonde air hostess who's on this flight.' The blonde air hostess at the back of the plane, realizing that the pilot had inadvertently left on the tannoy, hurried down the plane as quickly as she could. Unfortunately for her, halfway down the aisle she tripped and fell. As she was helped to her feet by a kind lady, the lady said, 'There's no need to rush, my dear. He said he was going to have a bath and a drink first.'   *(B.W.)*

Our first game that year was in the Transvaal, at over 6000 feet above sea level. The air was so thin that we were very short of breath. Ken Kennedy, the Irish hooker and doctor, had shown us some positions which opened up our lungs more fully in order to inhale as much air as possible. One of these entailed standing upright and holding our arms out sideways at shoulder height. We did this as often as possible. The first time was not long after the kick-off, when the pace of the game was frenetic. As we formed up for a line-out and the ball was being retrieved from the crowd, we all outstretched our arms and started inhaling as much as possible. As you can imagine, this brought quite a reaction from the crowd as well as some peculiar looks from our opposite numbers. One reporter was quoted the next day as saying that it was the only time during the game that the British Lions pack had been crucified.

(F.S.)

The British Lions party went to Kruger National Park for a few days rest midway through the tour. Quite a few of the boys were carrying injuries, including Phil Bennett, who had a nasty gash which required ten stitches to his ankle. On the first night there, the players had a good drink and a sing-song. We were in a large native-type hut. There was no electricity or modern amenities. The camp was dotted with small huts, with two players sleeping in each. When the party came to an end in the early hours of the morning and the players walked outside, they were confronted by a starless South African night, so black you could not see a hand in front of your face. Willie John McBride, who was sharing with Phil Bennett, decided to carry the injured Phil on his back, as Phil had great difficulty walking. A few minutes later, while we were still looking for each of our huts, there was a loud growl and a terrific scream. Everybody ran in all directions and, unfortunately for Phil, Willie John ran under a low-hanging branch of a tree. Missing Willie by inches, it caught Phil across his forehead and knocked him off Willie's back.

In the morning, when the Lions' manager came around the camp, he saw a dead baboon lying outside Willie and Phil's hut. Willie opened the door and the manager asked him, 'What's happened here?'

Phil Bennett poked his head out and his face was covered in dried blood.

The manager looked shocked. 'Well?' Phil looked at the baboon and then he turned to the manager. 'He didn't put up much of a fight,' said Phil.

We later learned that during the night a leopard had attacked the baboon, who had managed to get away only to die of his wounds, according to the Park Ranger. *(B.W.)*

Having won the first two Test matches, we went into the third with the prospect of being the first British Lions touring team ever to win a series in South Africa. The captain was Willie John McBride, the great Irish

second-row forward, and just before we took the field he lined up the whole team in the dressing room and, starting at the bottom and working his way right along the line, he thumped each member in the chest, calling out their name at the same time. It was his unsubtle way of finally bringing us all together. As I stood at the bottom of the line I braced myself for my captain's assault. He duly delivered a huge punch to my chest and called out my name. Unfortunately for me, he pivoted and turned round and hit me again. Now the real truth is out about why the kick-off for the third Test was delayed: I was recovering from my captain's assault in the dressing room. It is the only time in rugby history that the sponge man has had to leave the field and go into the dressing room to attend to a player prior to the kick-off.   *(G.B.)*

'... he saw a dead baboon lying outside Willie and Phil's hut.'

13

HOTELS

At the end of a tour of Britain by the all-conquering All Blacks, the New Zealanders had agreed to play France in Paris on their way home. The hotel where the All Blacks were staying had a famous chef, and this chef was determined that he was going to give Colin Meads, the legendary All Blacks forward, the greatest meal he had ever had. As soon as the All Blacks arrived, the head chef sought out Meads and said, 'Mr Meads, you are the greatest player in the world. I want you to enjoy the greatest chef in the world. What is your favourite dish?' Colin Meads thought for a moment and said, 'Steak – I want the biggest and best steak you have ever served.' The chef immediately replied, 'That is no problem. How do you like your steak?' Meads thought for another moment and then looked the chef straight in the eye. With a straight face he said, 'Knock off its horns, wipe its arse, and slap it on the plate!'   (B.W.)

Before a tour of New Zealand in 1971 the British Lions stayed one night in London, where we were kitted out with blazers, flannels, etc. That night I was to share a room with the one and only Willie John McBride, who by that time had become a legend in his own lifetime. Despite the fact that I had played against Willie John a couple of times at international level, he and I had not spoken often because I was still very much the young whippersnapper. When I got up to my bedroom with all my gear, the great man was already packed for New Zealand and was sitting up in bed in his pyjamas puffing his pipe. As I muddled about trying to get my bags packed, I was racking my brains for something to say to the great man – something he would not totally ignore. Nothing at all came to mind. Eventually the great man doubled my misery when he broke the silence with, 'Brownie, do you snore?' I was immediately petrified: I am renowned as being one of the worst snorers in the world. However, not wishing to concern the great man, I immediately replied, 'No, of course not, Willie. I won't disturb you for one moment.' I can hereby confirm absolutely that I did not disturb the great man's slumber for one minute that night because I sat up all night and read a book. Many people have said to me since what wonderful respect I showed. I can tell you all here and now it was no more than blind fear. *(G.B.)*

Roger Arneil was an incredible guy to share a room with. Sometimes he would frighten you out of your wits. One year, Nairn McEwan was sharing a Paris hotel room with Roger gaining his first cap for Scotland against France. On the eve of the match, Arneil, who had played for Scotland many times and who had toured with the Lions as well, was asked by his young room-mate for some inside information on the French players. 'What's this guy Dauga like?' asked McEwan casually. 'He is *huge*,' replied the seasoned campaigner. 'He's like a man mountain!' Nairn looked dismayed. 'Can't jump, then, can he?' said Nairn, looking hopeful. 'Jump?' retorted Roger incredulously. 'He could touch the *sky* if he felt like it!' There was a shocked silence as the young McEwan composed himself. 'Well, at least he's not that fast, then, is he?' said Nairn, playing his last trump. '*Fast?*' echoed Roger ominously. 'Fast? He's like greased lightning!' Nairn fell silent. He clambered sadly into his bed, and his head dropped on the pillow like a stone. Out of the darkness came Arneil's voice: 'Oh, Nairn,' added Roger helpfully, 'he's got hands like shovels as well.' And with that he turned over and went sound asleep. Nairn stared at the ceiling all night.

Arneil scared the living daylights out of many of his room-mates, because, quite apart from what he said before he went to sleep, there was also the question of his sleepwalking. Once, when I was sharing a room with him, I awoke to find the man sprinting on the spot beside his bed, shouting, 'Go – go – go – go – go!' at the top of his voice. He then tore across the room and crash-tackled a group of high-backed chairs. I jumped up and helped him to his feet – he was still fast asleep – and eventually got him back into his bed, where he settled for the rest of the night. Next morning, he obviously didn't remember a thing. 'I feel sore and stiff,' complained Arneil, puzzled. 'No bloody wonder,' I replied. *(G.B.)*

Following Scotland's victory over France at Murrayfield a while ago we returned to the North British Hotel in Edinburgh to start our celebrations. The champagne flowed and by the time we filtered through to dinner we were all well oiled. The first course was soup, and we all looked forward to getting a decent plate of the hot stuff inside us before launching into the heavy eating. Imagine our disgust when we put our first spoonsful to our mouth to discover it was stone cold! There were a lot of swilling and splurting noises, followed by spoons thrown down heavily in bowls, and then the waiter was loudly summoned. I demanded to know how long this bloody old swill had been sitting out on the tables, and said we'd like it hotted up, and pretty damn quick. 'Sir,' said the French waiter politely, 'Vichysoise eez served *always* cheeled.'   *(G.B.)*

In New Zealand the night before the North Auckland game I was awakened in my bedroom by a noise at the window. Two intruders were attempting to break in and the first was almost inside. I yelled at him and he immediately began clambering back out again, screaming to his accomplice, 'He is awake, he's awake.' In the pitch darkness I couldn't find my rugby boots to belt him with, but I quickly filled the litter bin with boiling water from the sink, and as they fled down the fire escape the water cascaded all over them. They dived into a car nearby and sped off into the night, not before I crashed the litter bin off the front windscreen of the car. I eventually got back into my room and slammed my window shut. As I was climbing into bed, there was a loud hammering on the door, and a voice I recognized as belonging to Derek Quinnell shouted, 'Keep the bloody noise down, will you? Some of us are trying to get some sleep!'   *(G.B.)*

During a British Lions tour to New Zealand I shared a room with Graham Price, the Welsh prop-forward. I found Graham to be the quietest roommate I had ever had on any of my tours. One morning at breakfast time I mentioned this to two or three of my team-mates and they all stated that they had found the same. We were soon joined by Bobby Windsor, the Welsh hooker, and we said to him, 'Bobby, when we room with Graham we found him really, really quiet. Now you're his clubmate and fellow countryman – when he's with you does he speak?' Bobby said,

'He then crash-tackled a group of high-backed chairs.'

'Speak! The last time I shared a room with him I had to check three
times in the one night to see if he was still breathing!'   *(G.B.)*

Following my suspension on the morning of the international between
Scotland and Wales, I played in Edinburgh for my club, West of Scotland,
against Stewarts Melville FP. To say that I found that game an anti-
climax compared with the international is an understatement. I did not
in fact stay in Edinburgh for the international, having decided instead
to watch it at home in Troon on television with some friends. Unfortunately, on my way back to Troon from Edinburgh, my car broke down in a
small village in the middle of Lanarkshire called High Blantyre. Hunting
feverishly for a television to watch the game, I eventually found a small
hotel and politely explained my predicament to the hotel manageress.
She apologized, saying that the only television was in the resident lounge
and it was already very busy. Just then a voice boomed out, 'Gordon
Brown, Bach, what are you doing here?' My eyes focused on a Welsh
supporter, completely bedecked in red and white scarf, rosette and
tammy. Instantly he whisked me into the lounge, where I was greeted
with an incredible sight. Dozens and dozens of Welshmen! All of them
up for the big game but not one of them with a ticket. I was given a
rapturous welcome by them all and a seat right in front of the television.
They had all been across to Edinburgh that morning to visit Murrayfield
and to walk the length of Princes Street; 'Just to take in the atmosphere
of the city.' The atmosphere they created inside that wee lounge in High
Blantyre made me feel as if I was *at* Murrayfield. The fact that they were
not actually at the match was of no significance whatsoever to them. 'It's
the trip we all love most,' they told me. 'The match itself isn't so important
to attend really. Mind you, we don't tell that to the wives!'   *(G.B.)*

On the night after the British Lions had won the third Test match in
South Africa, and therefore the series, we had a magnificent party in the
hotel. Eventually every single fire extinguisher in the hotel was let off,
but although a fire extinguisher is great while it is working it never lasts
for very long. That does not go for fire hoses, which are linked to the
main water main. The water from them just keeps on coming and coming
and coming. By the time the wee small hours dawned, the hotel was
awash with water. Our manager had gone to bed fairly early that night
and was therefore oblivious to the mayhem we were creating. He was

rudely awakened around 8 a.m. by the hotel manager who, of course, was remonstrating about the state of his hotel. When our team manager got up from bed and splashed his way through the water, he realized what the hotel manager was talking about. Eventually he waded up to Willie John McBride's room and went to knock at the door. But there was no door there. He waded into Willie John's room, and there was the great man sitting on his bed as it bobbed about on the water, puffing away at his pipe. The team manager went bananas. He screamed and bawled at Willie John that we were the worst touring team of all time. He said that we would all have to go home on the first available plane and that we would be the biggest disgrace to British rugby. At last Willie John said to him, 'Alan, do you mind if I ask you one question?' 'Yes, what is it?' the manager snapped. 'Is there anybody dead?'   *(F.S.)*

Following a British Lions match against the Barbarians at Twickenham the teams adjourned to the London Hilton Hotel for the dinner dance. During the dance there was a free bar for the players and wives. Some American gate-crashers found their way into our function, and one of the females found herself standing beside me in the crush at the bar which must have been about twelve deep. Catching sight of my kilt she turned to me and asked, 'Are you a true Scotsman?' Smiling at her, I gave her the normal standard reply to such a question: 'It's up to you to find out for yourself!' Without thinking, she immediately thrust her hand up my kilt! She let out a high-pitched shriek, which caught the attention of everybody in the room, despite the noise coming from the band, and then she pushed her way out of the crowd and disappeared from the room, never to be seen again! When I eventually got back to the table with the drinks from the bar, my wife smiled at me and said, 'Gordon, you'll have to stop wearing your sporran *under* your kilt!'   *(G.B.)*

On Scotland's tour of Argentina the team captain, Jim Telfer, was keen that none of us should suffer from sunburn; consequently he had banned sunbathing for the whole of the tour. We felt that we were being rather ill done by with this dictum from on high and during our stay in Rosario we were determined to catch up with some sunbathing – after all, the weather was quite magnificent. Our game against Rosario had been postponed because of some dreadful rioting taking place in the town and the police had announced a curfew. We were confined to our hotel. One

afternoon four or five of us decided to sneak up onto the flat roof of the hotel. From this vantage point we could see smoke spiralling up from the burnt-out building and smouldering buses, evidence of the rioting down below.

We had been stretched out on the roof sunning ourselves for about half an hour, listening to the sounds of distant gunfire and the buzz of a fast-approaching helicopter, when suddenly Jim Telfer burst onto the hotel roof screaming blue murder. We thought this was taking the sunbathing ban a bit seriously, but we soon discovered our mistake. 'For Chrissake get off this roof!' he yelled. 'That's a police helicopter looking for snipers and if they see you they'll bloody shoot you!'   *(G.B.)*

Following a Scotland–England rugby international at Twickenham the Scottish players had made their way back to the team hotel. It was around midnight and they were delighted to discover the restaurant in the hotel still open. Some of the players sat down to have something to eat. When he had eaten his starter Dave Rollo, the Scottish prop-forward, excused himself from the table because he wasn't feeling too well. He left the dining room looking slightly green about the gills, and returned after an interval, evidently having been violently sick. He resumed his seat at the table, and the main course arrived, which he ate with apparent relish. After a subdued silence, though, he quietly told his team-mates that he was feeling sick again, and disappeared in the direction of the men's room. The sweet was just being served when he came back, and to our suprise he tackled it, undeterred by his gastric experiences. After the cheese and biscuits, however, he was gone again, returning eventually to the dining room with a deathly pallor. Sitting down at the table, he smiled and patted his stomach. 'You know, boys,' he said 'after a rugby international, there's nothing like getting a good meal inside you.'
(G.B.)

During the Marr rugby club Easter tour to Whitley Bay, the club's new full-back was to share a hotel room with one of the second-row forwards. Now the second-row forward was renowned for his colossal snoring, and the young full-back, fearing that he would not get one minute's sleep

'. . . there was the great man sitting on his bed as it bobbed about on the water, puffing away at his pipe.'

during the night, struck on an idea. Just before putting the lights out in the bedroom he went across to the second-row forward's bed, kissed him on the cheek and said, 'Night, night.' He then climbed into bed and turned over and went to sleep, knowing full well that the second-row forward would not for one minute close his eyes. He slept undisturbed all night long.

(G.B.)

14
WIVES

Prior to the British Lions touring team being announced one year, Andy Irvine, the Scottish full-back, was unsure whether or not to go on the tour because his wife was due to have their first baby right in the middle of it. But, being a typical rugby player, Andy went on the tour. As his wife's date got closer and closer, Andy became more and more uptight. As I was friendly with him and went around with him a lot, I was getting as uptight as he was. His wife's date came and went, and still there was no news. After a few days, one night Brynmor Williams, the Welsh scrum-half, burst into my bedroom and said, 'Broonie, Broonie, Andy's wife's had the baby. Both well, no problems.' I was so relieved, then I thought: 'Andy – I must go and see him. I quickly jumped out of bed and sprinted away down the corridor (well, I ran as fast as I could ever run). Andy's door was two inches ajar. Without any subtlety I battered straight through the door, and there he was sitting hunched up on the bed with his back to me. I jumped on top of the bed, threw my arms round about him and started to bounce him up and down, screaming at the top of my voice, 'You beauty! It's fantastic news! She is brilliant! You're fantastic! What a guy!' and I shouted and screamed and bawled and bounced for fully a minute. When I released him, he turned round and said to me, 'Hey, Broonie, I'm on the phone.' He was doing a live interview on the local radio station.   *(G.B.)*

Jim Renwick played for Scotland many times in the centre and is certainly one of the finest ambassadors our sport has ever had. Off the field there is a nice quiet way to wee Jim. One night I was driving him,

his wife, Sheila, and my wife, Linda, from Hawick to Edinburgh. Halfway
to Edinburgh Jim suddenly sat forward and said to me, 'Quick, Broonie,
pull into the side of the road. Sheila is not feeling very well.' So I did so.
I jumped out of the car, put my seat forward and got Sheila out. Immediately she was sick, so I supported her and took her to the side of the road.
All the time she was being sick I kept looking over my shoulder watching
for wee Jim – but he never ever got out of the car. Eventually I helped
Sheila to clean up, got her back into the car and off we went to Edinburgh.
When I was on my own with Linda, I said how surprised I had been that
wee Jim had not come to help while his wife was being so sick. Linda
replied that she had been very surprised too. In fact at the time she had
turned round to wee Jim and said, 'Are you not getting out of the car
too?' and he had turned round and said, 'No. I'm feeling fine, thank you.'
                                                                    (G.B.)

When I played for Marr College FP in Troon one day my second-row
partner was late for the kick-off. 'I had a wee bit of trouble at home,' he
said. 'I'll explain after the game'. Over a pint later he told us about his
'wee bit of trouble'. As he was leaving his house, he had been confronted
by his girlfriend's irate husband. A fight broke out, the police were called,
and the husband was taken off in the 'meat wagon'. Going back into the
house, my second-row partner then called to his wife, 'I'll be off then,
love.' He found her standing in the hallway with their two children, bags
packed. 'I've had enough,' she said and his entire family marched down
the garden path towards his father-in-law's waiting car. My partner had
arrived in the dressing room literally one minute before we ran onto the
pitch, begging his captain's forgiveness. 'All right,' said the captain, 'but
don't make a habit of this.'   *(G.B.)*

When I played for my club side West of Scotland our captain, Quintin
Dunlop, was quite a character. After many years as a bachelor, Quintin
finally fell to the charms of the lovely Joan. Most of the team were at
Quintin's wedding. After the main reception Quintin was about to leave
the hotel to join Joan in the taxi to hasten off on their honeymoon. Some
of us decided to give Quintin a fond farewell that he would never forget.
He was kidnapped and hidden in a small bedroom. In the meantime one
of our clubmates, Chris Rea, who played centre for Scotland and the
British Lions, was duly stripped to his Y-fronts and carried out wrapped

in a sheet taken from a bed, with only his feet protruding. We carried Chris – or, as everyone else thought, Quintin – shoulder-high in this sheet through the throng out into the street and into the taxi. We told the taxi driver to set off immediately. Everyone, including Quintin's mother, was shouting fond farewells to Quintin and his new bride, Joan. Joan was making every effort to unwind Quintin from his wrappings, or at least get his head free, to acknowledge the fond farewells. She wasn't successful, as we'd done a good job in the packaging department, and Chris was holding the crucial parts of the sheet. Suddenly, though, she noticed something not to her liking, and let out a scream. 'This isn't Quintin!' she shrieked from the depths of the taxi, as we meanwhile, were urging the driver to make all speed to their honeymoon hideaway. Sadly, Joan's deafening cries eventually alerted the crowd. Our plot was uncovered – to reveal Chris Rea at the bottom of the bundle. How had the bride spotted the swop? Well, what Chris lacks in height he makes up for in other ways: size twelve feet!   *(G.B.)*

15

A LITTLE MISUNDERSTANDING

I was once honoured to be selected for the Cooptimists XV who were
going to play in the Bob Oakes Memorial match against Hartlepool
Rovers. This was especially gratifying for me because it was the first
invitation to play in a senior representative rugby match and it was a
fixture that my brother Peter had played in some years previously, with
great distinction. I journeyed down to Hartlepool with two Scottish internationals, Ian McLauchlan and Richard Allan. We arrived at the Hartlepool Rovers ground and joined in a welcoming reception. We were introduced to the Cooptimists president, George St Clair Murray. Richard
Allan was first to step forward and he said rather proudly, 'My name is
Richard Allan and I play for Hutchie rugby club and Scotland.' George
St Clair Murray replied, 'Well, congratulations on being selected for the
Cooptimists. Delighted to have you here, old boy.' Then the president
turned towards Ian McLauchlan, who stepped forward to shake his hand.
'My name is Gordon Brown,' said Ian, 'and I play for West of Scotland
and Scotland.' (The swine! I thought: now *I'll* have to say I'm *him!*) The
president beamed at McLauchlan: '*Gordon!* Delighted to have you with
the Cooptimists. We do, of course, know all about your big brother Peter,
and if you become half as good a player as he, then you will have done
quite admirably!' And then the president turned to me, inspecting me
rather carefully. 'Hello, Mr St Clair Murray,' I said, my confidence
suddenly draining into my boots. 'I'm – I'm Ian McLauchlan and I play
for Jordanhill and Scotland.' The president's face clouded. 'Jordanhill.

' "Are you gentlemen looking for a job?" '

Jordanhill?' he repeated, as if chewing over a particularly nasty obscenity. 'Well, I must speak to Dodds, the secretary, about this – we don't want the likes of *you* playing for the Cooptimists.'   *(G.B.)*

On one British Lions tour a player was telling us that he had been in trouble with the police on five or six occasions. We asked him what it was like to be in the dock and he replied that it was, obviously, pretty traumatic. Further inquiries about the outcome of the cases met with, 'Oh, three times I was found guilty and three times not guilty.' We asked about the times he was found guilty, and he replied that because he had a very good young lawyer he always managed to get off on appeal. When we enquired about the costs involved in all this, he admitted that it had cost him quite a bit of money; in fact, his lawyer, although a young fellow, was very wealthy. In fact, said the player, 'He already has two Rolls Royces.' Then, after a slight pause and a stroke at his chin, he added, 'Mind you, one of them is a re-spray.'   *(B.W.)*

After a British Lions tour fixture in Rhodesia, which the Lions had won, there was a function at the Rhodesian Police club. Later on in the evening the then Prime Minister, Ian Smith, came to make a speech. Shortly after this Dick Milliken and I decided to go back to the hotel. Just outside the entrance to the club was parked a beautiful black-tinted-window Cadillac. Being slightly under the influence, we decided to take the opportunity to have a ride in a Cadillac. After driving around for only five or ten minutes, the partition behind the front seats slid across and the Prime Minister said, 'Are you gentlemen looking for a job?'   *(F.S.)*

In 1986 I attended a rugby club dinner in the United Arab Emirates. The day after the dinner there was a special rugby challenge match between a Saudi XV and a Gulf XV. Midway through the first half one of the Saudi players hurt his knee. After a moment or two the Gulf XV hooker went across to survey the damage to this poor fellow. Having quickly examined the knee he said, 'This could actually be quite serious. I'm a doctor. I think you should go off.' The player was very reluctant, as he was one of the star men of the Saudi XV, but he nevertheless did not want to cause any permanent damage, so off he went.

The Gulf team went on to win. It was bad enough for the Saudis to see their lead rapidly eroded. It was bad enough to finish the game with only fourteen men. But it was extremely infuriating to learn in the bar afterwards that the Gulf captain was a plumber not a doctor. Talk about adding insult to injury. *(G.B.)*

Two of Hawick rugby club's most famous players were the centres Alistair Cranston and Jim Renwick. Their styles were in total contrast, but they complemented each other. In one of their club matches at Hawick, Alistair Cranston was lining up to drop a goal when Jim Renwick screamed at him, 'No! No!' Cranston reacted immediately, thinking that a move was afoot, and threw the ball to Jim Renwick. Renwick promptly dropped a goal. *(G.B.)*

Shortly after the independence of Zimbabwe, Public School Wanderers played the national side in Harare. The Zimbabwe side, having played well in the early part of the first half of the game, were overrun comprehensively in the second half. In the midst of this, one of the supporters, clearly not fully clued up about independence, roared out, 'Come on, Rhodesia, you're playing like a crowd of bloody Zimbabweans!!' *(F.S.)*

One year the British Lions side played in Rhodesia. The Lions hooker that day was Ken Kennedy, the Irishman, and he became quite upset at the number of squint put-ins which the Rhodesian scrum-half was getting away with. Ken Kennedy's patience finally burst and, after one particularly bad put-in from the Rhodesian scrum-half, as the scrum broke up he ran past the referee, saying to him, 'I have never come across a referee in my entire career quite so much in need of a white stick and a guide dog as you, sir.' The referee sprinted after him, grabbed his arm and shouted, 'What did you just say to me?' Kennedy turned and said, 'Christ, don't tell me you're deaf too!' *(F.S.)*

16

NUDE IN
NEW ZEALAND

On the morning following the Lions second Test victory in New Zealand we had a fabulous party. It started off with the team manager wakening every single one of us with a compulsory double whisky. There followed a hearty sing-song in his room, along with a lot of good banter and stories. After two hours it was noticed that one of our players was missing. The big Irish second-row forward, Moss Keane, stated that he knew where the culprit was: next door with his girlfriend. I immediately despatched Moss to bring the offender back to the group; remembering Moss's nickname of Rent-a-storm, I advised him to open the doors properly. We listened to the slight kerfuffle in the room next door to us and eventually our room door opened and in came Moss Keane. Under his arm was our team-mate, completely starkers and squirming like a wee tadpole. Under Moss's other arm was the girlfriend, completely starkers and squirming like a wee tadpole. Mossy stood in the doorway with his load under each arm and shouted to me, 'To be sure, Broonie, did you be wanting the two of them?'   (G.B.)

During the 1974 Lions tour of New Zealand we travelled to two different cities each week. The journeying became rather tedious and some of the players hated the movement to and fro between the cities. Following the third Test match in Port Elizabeth, we all piled into the plane at the airport on the Sunday morning to fly up the coast to East London. I was sitting in the plane beside Fergus Slattery, whose attention was

'Mossy stood in the doorway with his load under each arm,'

consumed by the newspapers. We no sooner had taken off from Port Elizabeth than I became aware that the plane was circling out over the sea and failing to make headway north towards East London. The pilot told us over the tannoy that due to a technical hitch he was having to shut down the starboard engine and we would be returning to Port Elizabeth immediately. The rest of my team mates and I were rather shocked at this, and we circled for some time over the sea, obviously dumping as much fuel as possible. At last the plane landed safely with a bit of a bump on Port Elizabeth runway and taxied to the airport terminal. We all breathed a huge sigh of relief at being safely back on *terra firma.* As the plane drew up outside the terminal building, Fergus Slattery lifted his nose out of his newspapers, stretched his arms, and sighed. 'Bobby,' he said, 'doesn't every stop on this tour look like the bloody one we just left!'   *(B.W.)*

On tours to New Zealand we went to the cinema regularly. One film we saw was *Survive,* based on a true story about an Argentinian rugby team whose plane crashed in the Andes. The players who survived the crash, in order to live until they were rescued, had to eat their dead team-mates. It was a stupid film for us to see because twice a week we were flying backwards and forwards across the Southern Alps in New Zealand. There was a very touching scene when the six survivors are picked up by helicopter and flown into Buenos Aires airport. The terminal building was crammed with people waiting to see the survivors arrive home safely. Of course nobody knew who had lived and who had died, but word of the cannibalism had gone ahead of them. As the six players came out of the helicopter they had about three hundred yards of tarmac to cross to reach the terminal building and their team coach – he had not been on the plane that crashed. The coach could not wait until the six had walked the three hundred yards so he burst out of the terminal building and sprinted all the way across the tarmac. As they walked past him, the camera zoomed straight in and focused on the coach's face. He was trying to say something and, although his lips were moving, there was nothing coming out. Steve Fenwick, the Welsh centre, shouted out, 'Which one of you buggers ate my stand-off?'

That night, when we were in the hotel getting our supper, Billy Beaumont was up pouring himself a cup of coffee – and of course Bill Beaumont has the biggest backside that has ever taken the pitch in international rugby. As he was getting his supper organized, Steve Fenwick shouted to him, 'You know, Bill, if our plane ever does crash in the Southern Alps, I hope you die, for I reckon we could survive for at least a month on your backside.'   *(B.W.)*

In 1977 Willie Duggan played number 8 for the Lions against a Maori team. It was a very tough match and some of the rucks were quite physical. At one stage Willie Duggan was trapped at the bottom of a ruck and one or two players were seen to aim boots at his head. He nevertheless got up and carried on with the game. Later I asked him if he had been aware of the pounding his head was taking. 'Yes,' he replied, 'I heard it.'   *(B.W.)*

One day on the tour we visited Auckland Zoo. As we walked round, we heard much hilarity coming from the direction of the monkey cage. On further investigation we discovered two monkeys copulating. As we stood watching in admiration a schoolteacher came across with about thirty or so children. The children immediately began giggling when they caught sight of the copulating monkeys. The mistress was rather embarrassed and initially didn't know what to do. She then called out, 'Quick, somebody, throw them a biscuit.' Steve Fenwick shouted out to the schoolmistress, 'If *you* were doing *that* and someone threw *you* a biscuit, would you stop?'   *(B.W.)*

The British Lions were touring New Zealand and one of their second-row forwards on the tour was David Marques. Now David was a proper English gentleman and during one of the Test matches an All Blacks forward trampled all over him. David very quickly jumped to his feet. Everyone, the forward included, expected David to smack him right on the nose but he proffered his hand in a friendly gesture. The All Black forward was quite taken aback and, slowly getting to his feet, felt obliged to shake hands with his victim – they then both ran off to continue the game. Once the game was over Don's team mates quizzed him over his reaction. 'I knew I couldn't hurt him by punching him,' said David, 'so instead I just wanted him to feel a proper cad.'   *(F.S.)*

I remember during a British Lions tour in New Zealand asking Barry John how much he owed to Gareth Edwards's long spin pass. He replied that Gareth's pass was fabulous because it gave him so much time and room to indulge himself. He added, 'Gareth's pass is now getting so long and accurate I just rubberstamp it "approved" on its way past.' Was he worried, I inquired, that Gareth took a bit of time to wind up before unleashing the ball? 'No,' Barry replied nonchalantly. 'You can't rush perfection, see.'

(B.W.)

When I was in New Zealand on the Lions tour one year I was making my way back to the team hotel in Wellington when I passed by a church. There was a giant poster outside the church stating, 'All ye tired of sinning hasten inside.' Underneath someone had scribbled, 'If not, please telephone Wellington 2379.'

(B.W.)

On another of our trips to the cinema in New Zealand we went to see one of the Dracula films. Just as Dracula was about to sink his teeth into the young lady's neck, Ian McLauchlan, the Scottish prop, sat forward and jammed two fingers into the side of Sean Lynch, the Irish prop-forward's, neck. Sean got the fright of his life and immediately erupted, yelling like a stuffed pig. He scrambled over the two rows in front of him, clambering all over the people sitting there and, screaming blue murder, ran out of the cinema. That night, when we were back in the hotel having our supper, Gareth Edwards told us not to go to bed before Sean, and he then disappeared. Eventually Sean went to bed and we all tiptoed down the corridor and listened outside his door. A few moments later we heard Sean screaming and all of a sudden his bedroom door came out on top of us with Sean scrambling over it, over the top of us and away down the corridor. We looked inside the bedroom and saw his wardrobe door swinging open. Further inspection found Gareth Edwards inside the wardrobe with a white sheet over his head; his false teeth were out so that all you could see were his two eye-teeth: a brilliant replica of Dracula. Gareth had to keep out of Sean's way for the next fortnight.

(F.S.)

In New Zealand we were in the team room one evening having a chat about the types of jobs we each did. Mike Gibson explained that he was a solicitor in Belfast. One of the boys asked him what was the most

'. . . a brilliant replica of Dracula.'

difficult case he had ever had to defend in court. Mike replied, 'That of a company director who was up on a charge of putting Green Shield stamps on his employees' insurance cards.' Mike said it was particularly difficult to defend because there in the court room were 10,000 insurance cards produced in evidence, all practically filled with Green Shield stamps. Mike's client was of course found guilty. The judge gave him a six-month suspended sentence. Plus an electric kettle.   *(F.S.)*

The Lions coach in New Zealand, Carwyn James, decided one day that the backs should go on a three-mile run to try to increase their stamina. One of the superstars of the tour, the Welsh stand-off, Barry John, was not enamoured of the prospect. After the players had set out on the run he fell back and very soon found himself fifty yards behind the group. So it was with some surprise that the rest of the players arrived panting back at the stadium to find Barry sitting with his feet up eating oranges. He'd got a lift on a lorry.   *(F.S.)*

We suffered many cocktail parties in New Zealand, attended by people who knew somebody who knew somebody else who possibly knew a bit about rugby but not much. We regularly switched our name tags, and nobody registered the difference. I would parade about with 'Gerald Davies' or 'Gareth Edwards' on my lapel, talking Welsh gibberish, while Gerald Davies would be over the other side of the room sporting 'Gordon Brown' on his jacket, telling everyone how he enjoyed being lifted in the line-out, otherwise how was he supposed to win the ball, and so on. One of these mind-bogglingly dull affairs followed a particularly gruelling journey between far-flung towns, and all we wanted to do was eat and get to bed. Imagine our horror when we discovered we had to mix with the local fans and dignitaries for at least a couple of hours before we were to get any food. It was Barry John who came to the rescue, secretly slipping into the kitchen and bribing the chef to fix up some steaks. One by one we were given the nod, eased into the kitchen, ate our steaks and left by the fire escape. When the welcoming speeches to the British Lions began, we were all snoring contentedly in our beds. The following morning our antics were front-page news, and the team manager gave us all a good dressing-down. What upset him more than anything was that he hadn't been called out for the steak and the fire escape. *(G.B.)*

Following our victory in the first Test in New Zealand we visited the holiday town of Queenstown for a few days' relaxation. One of the relaxations on offer was deerstalking. Willie John McBride, the great Irish second-row forward, had been in Queenstown on the previous Lions tour in 1966 but had spent a rather unfortunate day without even *spotting* a stag, never mind *shooting* one!

When we arrived at the small farm in the foothills, we were introduced to the deerstalkers.

One old guy said to Willie John, 'I remember you from '66. You had a very unfortunate day, you didn't even see a stag.' Willie John grumbled in the affirmative. The old guy went on, 'You come with me today, and I will guarantee you all the stag that you want!' Off went Willie John.

We were all paired with one stalker each and, at about 7 a.m., set off in different directions up into the hills. The plan was to stay out on the hills for as long as necessary, and the only food we had was bars of chocolate. We were so excited about the day's outing that food was not a priority. My stalker was George McBride from Southland, Willie John's cousin. He took me all over the lower hills that day and we stalked five or six stag, but unfortunately each time I fired I missed! George's patience seemed inexhaustible; despite all his stalking efforts, I always seemed to be blowing the situation. When it neared 5 p.m. George turned to me and said, 'Well, Gordon, we had better start heading back down to the valley to our rendezvous point at the farmhouse.' I was disappointed that I had not bagged anything, and I think George was a bit disappointed too, but he hid it well. We were soaked to the skin because it had rained non-stop for the whole day.

As we neared the farmhouse, looking across to the right in the middle of an open grass field, I spied a huge stag. It seemed somewhat ironic that we had spent all day up in the hills crawling about, at times on all-fours, trying to find a stag, when lo and behold here was one right in the middle of a green field, barely a quarter of a mile from the farmhouse.

George said to me, 'Do you fancy having a go at it?'

I said, 'Of course I do.'

He said, 'Well, we will have to circle away round behind it to get downwind, otherwise it will sense us.'

This took fully half an hour. Slowly but surely crawling on all-fours, I moved to within a hundred yards of the beast. I settled into a shooting position and, with George whispering last-second instructions in my ear, and with the beast in my sights, I squeezed the trigger. Bang! The sound of the rifle shot rang out round the valley. The animal jumped into the air, then keeled over, stone-dead. I immediately jumped to my feet screaming, 'Yaahoo, you beauty!' Such was my excitement.

All of a sudden, from about thirty yards away to my right, Willie John McBride's voice boomed out, *'Brown, you bastard.'* There was the great man shaking his huge fist in my direction as he thundered his way through the undergrowth towards me. Unbeknown to me, Willie John had been up the mountain, down the mountain, and round the mountain three times, and in the whole day had never even *spied* a stag, never mind *shot* at one! Eventually, sodden with rain, he had made his way back to the farm. Following a nice hot bath and getting into his dry clothing he had been watching for us coming down the roadway back to the farm when he spied the stag in the middle of the field in the same way I had done. Donning his sodden gear once again, he had circled to get downwind of the stag – in the opposite direction to the way George and I had done! He actually had the stag in his sights and was about to squeeze the trigger, when I shot the bloody thing from underneath his nose! He was not impressed with my timing.   *(G.B.)*

17

TIR NA N'OG

How come Irish rugby players have such long careers? To name but a few: Millar, McBride, O'Reilly, McLoughlin, Flynn, Kiernan, Orr, Gibson. Is it good clean living patterns? Doubtful. Maybe it's just their insatiable appetites. Unlikely. The secret may be entwined in Irish folklore and Tir Na N'Og – the land of everlasting youth. Whatever the reason, no other country has succeeded in turning out a geriatric brigade with such aplomb. Moss Keane and I had the dubious pleasure of sharing this mantle when, in 1974, along with McBride, Kennedy, McLoughlin and many other old hands, we won the championship. That side was branded by the press 'Dad's Army'. In 1975 many of the war horses retired and a new side emerged. It was therefore potentially very embarrassing for both Moss Keane and myself to be playing in a Five Nations champion-ship-winning side in 1982, eight years after the success of 'Dad's Army'. The international press revived the same tag for the Irish side. Mossie and myself said naught and the storm passed on, possibly because Mossie caused such havoc in that championship run. He succeeded in confusing everybody on the Park, and possibly elsewhere, as he spent most of the afternoon pushing in the line-outs and jumping in the scrums!

One of the essential ingredients of the rugby circus is humour and the telling and retelling of stories. Inevitably with each telling they grow taller, and often fiction becomes fact. Ireland has been no laggard in this arena.

Kilkenny, situated in the south-east of Ireland, is a free city, taking its charter from James I in 1609. It is a place of great charm, steeped in history and with a proud tradition in the arts and many cultural

activities. At first sight, therefore, it may appear a strange place for
Willie Duggan to inhabit, notwithstanding the fact that the city does
have its distractions, including one of the finest breweries in Ireland.
Willie is a man of purpose, always committed and unrelenting in the
attainment of his goal, and therein lies the reason why he finds solace
in this charming city.

For Willie, Kilkenny is strategically well placed, seventy-five miles
away from his club, Blackrock College RFC, his province of Leinster and
the Irish Rugby Football Union. Therefore his closest training ground
has never been nearer than seventy-five miles away. He has thus been
able to enjoy a carefree existence, far from the shrills of the trainer's
whistle, in an environment where he can easily contemplate his next
move.

There are, however, many who believe that Willie quietly organized
clandestine training sessions for himself. If this was so, then the secrecy
must have been so intense that he either forgot when he was to train, or
where, thus conserving his energy for an all-out assault on match day.

The 150-mile return journey always proved to be an excellent excuse
for avoiding training sessions. Blackrock College RFC in their wisdom
decided many years ago that, if it was not possible to bring the horse to
the water, then they would bring the water to the horse. It was agreed
by all the 1st XV, including Willie, that a training session in Kilkenny
was the only way to get the full squad together for a much needed run-
out. After a typical Saturday game the players drove down the following
morning to Kilkenny to train. Arriving at the practice ground, they were
not surprised to find that Willie had not arrived. Concern arose, however,
when some forty-five minutes elapsed and Willie had still not appeared.
The Duggan house was inspected; Willie was not in the bed and there
were no tell-tale signs of his presence. The training session for the squad
went ahead without Willie, and no sooner had it ended than he appeared.
The inquiry was opened. 'Where were you, Willie?' 'I was in Dublin,' he
replied. Ah, Dublin indeed: still seventy-five miles away from the nearest
training ground.

Tenacity, courage and strength were the hallmarks of Willie Duggan's
game. Like the rest of us, he was human, and I remember vividly a game
in Cape Town in 1982 when we played for the President's XV against

' "That little bastard has been following me around all afternoon." '

Western Province at Newlands. Everything had gone wrong and we were
being hammered by the Curry Cup holders. Willie approached a ruck in
the latter stages of the game and I noticed him standing on a snail and
crushing it with the heel of his boot. I asked him what the hell he was
doing and he grumbled, 'That little bastard has been following me around
all afternoon.'

The first time I recall seeing one of our elder statesmen, Syd Millar,
was as a youngster in the fourpenny seats in my local cinema. The
Newsreel was reporting on the prowess of the four countries' celebration
game at Twickenham in 1959. An awesome sight appeared in the midst
of celluloid; it looked like a Sumo wrestler wearing a scrumcap. With
ball in hand Syd Millar was powering his way like a sprinting buck from
thirty yards out to score. untouched by human hand, between the posts.
A star was born. If Syd Millar had at that time imagined that he would
still be engaged in international rugby almost three decades later, he
would have voluntarily committed himself to a home for the bewildered.
Yet he went on to attain thirty-seven caps for Ireland, coach and
manager, and he also led Ireland's charge in the inaugural World Cup
in the Antipodes.

Like all players, Syd had to serve his apprenticeship. In one of his
early assignments, against the French at Lansdowne Road, the then
coach, captain, medical officer and physiotherapist, Wiggs Mulcahy,
exhorted his team-mates in the dressing room to annoy, upset and distract
the French from the kick-off. The master plan was to upset the Latin
temperament. In the first scrum all hell broke loose. The only casualty
was Millar, who was found prostrate on the ground. Wiggs inquired what
ailed him. Millar's reply was short: 'The bastard bit me.' 'Get up, Syd,
and get into the next scrum and bite him back.' Millar replied, 'Wiggs,
I can't. I've left my teeth in the dressing room.'

As Syd grew older, the half-time break became a sanctuary for rest
and recuperation. Charlie McCorry brought out the tray of oranges, the
bottle of water, holy and otherwise, but Millar demanded honey. Yes,
honey. It's not particularly remarkable, therefore, that some devastating
wit landed him with the nickname of Yogi Bear.

I first played in the green shirt with Syd in 1970, a year which marked
his recall from exile, paving the way for other notable has-beens, such
as Tony O'Reilly and, a year later, Ray McLoughlin. On the playing field
Ireland recorded two handsome victories against Scotland and Wales at

Lansdowne Road, albeit with Syd Millar, the oldest international rugby player in the world. At the end of that season, Syd went to Argentina with Ireland. In Rosario an unfortunate incident occurred when the local flanker kicked Ronnie Lamont as he lay on the ground. Millar immediately set upon the Rosario flanker, who turned on his heels and ran. Syd chased him relentlessly, even though for every ten yards the flanker covered Syd was only covering five. The unfortunate referee also joined in the chase, which was brought to a conclusion only when Millar collapsed from physical exhaustion.

Syd and his close companion, neighbour and club-mate for many years, Willie John McBride, were both involved in an incident on that tour which fully tested their faith in and loyalty to each other. On the eve of a training session, the Irish party were invited to an Argentinian-style barbecue. Syd was relishing his second or third portion of the local delicacy. When he asked what the meat was, he was told by one of his local hosts that it was 'bulls' balls'. Millar gasped and sighed, but worse was to follow. The following morning the team had a tough training session. The scrummaging practice was fierce and McBride, packing behind Millar, got the surprise of his life. All of a sudden the scrum broke up. The dreaded Montezuma's revenge had struck the hapless Millar – McBride was never again to break from the scrum with such alacrity and speed. *(F.S.)*

I was invited to Ballymena rugby club in Northern Ireland to take part in the Tom Kiernan's XV against the Ballymena club side which included Willie John McBride. The captain of Tom Kiernan's XV, despite Tom's presence in the team, was none other than Fergus Slattery, Ireland's magnificent wing-forward. We rendezvoused two hours before the kick-off at a hotel in Ballymena. The first part of the build-up to the game was two compulsory double whiskies and a plate of ham sandwiches. We then set off for the ground. For this match there was no warm-up. There were no tactics. There were no codes of any kind for the line-outs, for the scrums, or the backs. My fear was that I had come all the way to Northern Ireland to take part in a game that would prove a shambles. How wrong I was! Never have I played in such an exhilarating game of rugby. Because nobody knew what anyone else was doing, *everything* was played off the cuff. The reaction from the players was devastating, and the crowd that night enjoyed a great game. The final score was something like 44 points to 42 in our favour. Did we discover that night the real recipe for successful enjoyable rugby? *(G.B.)*

One year the Scottish team went over to Dublin to play Ireland. When we got off the plane and onto the bus at Dublin airport, the bus driver, rather an aged gentleman, told us what an honour it was to drive us to our hotel, the Shelbourne. It was always a bonus for the driver of the year to take the international teams into the city centre. Just before we set off from the airport, one of the two police outriders who were to escort us into the city centre came onto the bus and said to this dear old gentleman, 'Whatever happens, you must follow us and don't stop for anything until we get to the Shelbourne Hotel.' The blood visibly drained from his face and he exclaimed, 'Be Jesus!'

Off we set. At first the bus journey was quite pleasant, but as we got nearer the city centre the speed increased rather than decreased. We crashed every red light en route and each time we did so the bus driver shouted, 'Be Jesus!' We entered O'Connell Street, where four lanes go one way and four lanes go the other. We were met by four blocked lanes in front of us. The two outriders bumped across the central reservation waving the bus driver to follow. Exclaiming, 'Be Jesus! Be Jesus!' he bounced us across the reservation. We then set off down O'Connell Street, heading against four lanes of oncoming traffic. The old bus driver put one hand up over one eye and cursed again. We watched amazed as one of the outriders stood up on his bike and parted the oncoming traffic as Moses did the Red Sea.

Fifteen more 'Be Jesus's' later, we came out the other end of O'Connell Street, and as we turned left into a narrower street one of the police outriders attempted to overtake us on the inside – and was duly struck by the bus.

Our bus driver looked down in horror, his lips forming the words 'Be' and then 'Jesus' as he tumbled from his seat to attend the stricken policeman. He was immediately hustled back into his vehicle as the other outrider frantically waved the bus on.

Eventually, and not without a few more oaths, we reached the Shelbourne Hotel. Leaping out of the bus, our driver grabbed one of the outriders. 'Be Jesus!' he shouted. 'What was all that about?'

The outrider said, 'We were just a bit concerned about the international team's security. That was why we didn't want them to stop anywhere.'

The driver exclaimed (you've guessed it), 'Be Jesus!'

We invited him into our hotel . . . for a drink; he was delighted to accept. As we entered the lobby we were frisked by the armed security guard. 'Oh! Be Jesus,' said the bus driver, feelingly. In he came and sat down, but before he would touch any of the Guinness that was poured for him he asked 'When do you boys come back here again?' We told him it would be in two years' time. A huge grin came over his face and he picked up his Guinness and downed it in one. Still grinning, he turned to us with a twinkle in his eye: 'Thanks be to Jesus, I'll be retired by then.'   *(G.B.)*

Most rugby players would never consider having a cigarette just prior to taking the field, especially in an international. But not so for Irish number 8, Willie Duggan. One of the last acts that Willie always performed before he took the field was stubbing out his cigarette. In one match in Dublin, when Ireland were playing France, Willie did his usual, but unfortunately it was slightly later than normal and as he came out of the dressing-room door to run down the tunnel he took one last drag at his cigarette. Not knowing what to do with the dog-end as he got to the top of the tunnel, he handed it to the referee of the day, Alan Hosie, who was making his debut in Dublin. Hosie's immediate reaction was to take the cigarette, not knowing what it was. Then he watched Willie Duggan run down the tunnel ahead of him – Willie always liked to go out last of the Irish team. There was a TV camera situated halfway down the tunnel. As Duggan went past the camera, he turned round and blew his smoke in Alan Hosie's direction. Just as Hosie came into camera shot, there was a puff of smoke and the viewers at home saw him holding a cigarette; so they all thought that Alan Hosie's last act prior to taking the rugby field for his first international in Dublin was to have a cigarette.
                                                      (F.S.)

It was a Wolfhounds against Killarney match, and the Wolfhounds got togged out in an adjoining dressing room to the Killarney team. There was very orderly and quiet preparation in the Killarney dressing room until the referee asked the Killarney side to take the field. Whereupon the Killarney captain roared at his team in a frenzy. 'Lads, I have only two words to say to you: A – ttack!'   *(F.S.)*

An Irish Lions player just returned from tour arrived back in his club house and was being quizzed by his team-mates, many of whom regarded him as being very tight with his money. He had been overjoyed with the tour. It was fantastic, the hospitality great, an abundance of drink, food, women, everything. As they got down to more precise details, one of the players asked him, 'How much was a pint of beer?' He said, 'God, I don't know'. Another player from the background roared up, 'That's two countries you don't know the price of beer in.'   *(F.S.)*

In the sixties there was a certain destructive element within touring parties culminating in the 'Wreckers and the Kippers' (players who chose to go on the rampage and those who chose to sleep) of the 1968 Lions tour to South Africa. Some players then were to officialdom what Long John Silver was to tap dancing. But a more serious approach in every respect was to emerge in the early seventies with the Lions tour to New Zealand. The professional approach by Carwyn James to his charges and the assistance which he got from a number of the senior players bore fruit in the first Test series victory for the Lions. In 1974 the Millar–McBride combination went into full swing, taking to South Africa the professional approach adopted by the 1971 Lions. Once again the reward was real, and the success can be measured in the results: undefeated on tour and an emphatic victory over the Springboks. The days of 'Wreckers and Kippers' were definitely over.   *(F.S.)*

The nearest the 1974 Lions tour came to controversy was in East London. In the early hours of the morning a couple of players were disturbed in their room by a few late-night revellers returning to base. The manager of the hotel went upstairs to keep the peace. Two players, clad in towels, were wandering along the hotel corridor when the vexed manager told them to go to their rooms. They refused, taking umbrage at his abrupt manner. The manager's threat to get the police fell on deaf ears, and he stormed off. As he approached the lift, the doors opened and out came the captain, Willie John McBride. The manager hurriedly explained to Willie John that he was on his way to get the police as he was unable to get a positive response from his players. McBride said nothing. The

'Some players then were to officialdom what Long John Silver was to tap dancing.'

manager marched into the lift. McBride beckoned him with a tilt of his head. The manager, with a sigh of relief, believing that order would be restored, stepped forward. McBride bent down to the diminutive manager and asked in a whisper, 'How many are you going to get?'   *(F.S.)*

In the early sixties Micky English played many games for Ireland at outside half. In one encounter against England the Irish took a heavy beating. Micky English's counterpart was the elusive Horicks-Taylor. In the dressing room after the game, English explained his feelings and possibly the feelings of his team-mates when he described how Horicks-Taylor ran at him for an England try. 'It was desperate stuff, lads, Horicks went one way, Taylor went the other and I was left holding the hyphen.'   *(F.S.)*

18

THE WORLD CUP

INNOCENT MARIO

It was particularly cruel and thoughtless of the organizers of the inaugural World Cup to stage the vast majority of matches in New Zealand. The All Blacks needed to be handicapped, not given a head start against inferior opponents who never recovered from jet lag and New Zealand hospitality. On the field it was inhospitable.

The All Blacks would have won the Webb Ellis Trophy had the competition been held in the Gobi Desert. Before a boot went in, the bookmakers had made the All Blacks 6–5 favourites and, as it turned out, the odds were not ungenerous.

It was clear from the kick-off that nothing short of the SAS was going to stop New Zealand from displaying the World Cup on its mantelpiece. It was etched into the face of Mario Innocenti, the noble captain of Italy, after his country had been hammered 70–6 at Eden Park, Auckland, in the opening game.

Innocenti occupies a footnote in the history of the game of Rugby Union Football. He was responsible for the first score in the first World Cup when he conceded a penalty try at a scrum near the Italian line. Italy needed that like a kick in the teeth, which they subsequently got.

There are those who felt that Mario was innocent, OK? 'We played well when we had some balls in the first half,' said Innocenti, whose English is not word-perfect. Presumably he was talking about possession. There again, perhaps not.

The score represented a world record, but a week later the All Blacks, much to the delight of the Italian press, scored even more against the second XV of Fiji, who were quite content to be away from home while their country was going through turmoil.

ALL ADS UP

The All Blacks were captained by David Kirk, who is extremely sharp in mind and body. He may look like a choirboy but there is nothing angelic about a New Zealand captain. Andy Dalton, who looks more like a cowboy than a choirboy, was originally chosen as the World Cup captain but was troubled by a hamstring injury before a game was played and Kirk was promoted.

This was just as well. Although Dalton did not play, he was never off the television screens in New Zealand and Scotland, for one, were sick of the sight of him.

Dalton, a farmer, starred in a commercial for a Japanese mini tractor (it wouldn't have stood up to the All Blacks' front row) and was filmed riding over the range like a mechanical choirboy, sorry cowboy. The Scots objected on the grounds that it infringed Rugby Union's amateur status and, although Dalton protested that neither he nor his tractor received a dollar, the organizing committee of the World Cup saw to it that the commercial was withdrawn while the competition was in progress.

Dalton wasn't the only star to lose his Equity card. We had a potential Oscar winner in Wayne Shelford, the best number 8 to punch his weight, who appeared in a colourful advertisement for paint. To the tune of Rod Stewart's 'Sailing', they managed to include the lyrics: 'We will bash the Frogs and thrash the Welsh.' The commercial should have been for whitewash because the scriptwriter, although short on subtlety, was extremely accurate in his prediction of All Black magic. Nor did it end there. You couldn't open a newspaper without seeing an All Black, singular or plural, promoting something and John Kirwan, who could stand on the right wing in New Zealand and win an election, cleverly substituted his father Pat in a full-page advertisement for a medicament to ease aching bones. It's about the only time John Kirwan has been

'John Kirwan . . . cleverly substituted his father Pat in a full-page advertisement for a medicament to ease aching bones.'

stopped from doing anything, although it has to be said that his father was a sound replacement. He looked a more suitable case for treatment.

AN ALL BLACK STUFFING

Steve McDowell, the All Blacks' tighthead prop, managed to escape the blackout. Unless John Kendall-Carpenter and the rest of the World Cup organizers went into a chemist's shop (presumably there was no need for such a fit body of men to do so), they would not have seen McDowell in all his glory. He appeared as a cardboard cutout – in Charles Atlas pose, for he is a former New Zealand judo champion – promoting a body-building nutrient.

The front row, remember, was considered to be the Achilles of the All Blacks' heel. One of the most revealing statements in the competition came from David Young, the 19-year-old Swansea prop who was minding his own business in Australia when he received a call that he was wanted by Wales. Young, who was in a bar, downed his can of Foster's, dived straight in against England in the quarter-finals in Brisbane and emerged a hero in a 16–3 victory. The bad news was that Wales had to face the All Blacks in the semi-finals.

Young, with the courage and blind faith of the young at heart, remarked: 'I watched McDowell against Scotland and Iain Milne, one of the best tight heads in the game who destroyed every front row in the Five Nations Championship, didn't know whether he was coming or going. He was blitzed. I haven't had a stuffing yet and I wouldn't like it to happen in the semi-finals of the World Cup.'

Wales, of course, got the stuffing of their lives but then so did everybody who came into contact with the All Blacks. At least Jonathan Davies had the satisfaction of providing the most unorthodox captain's speech. Against Canada at Invercargill Wales played in green to avoid a colour clash and after the match they did not carry out the tradition of exchanging jerseys.

'We can get a lot of money for flogging our jerseys back home,' explained Davies in his inaugural speech as captain of his country.

The Canadians were bemused, the Wales management buried their heads in their hands and a few pips from the top brass, like Kendall-Carpenter and Bob Weighill, the secretary of the International Board, were not amused. Davies, of course, was joking although the green jerseys were rather exclusive. They would cost an arm and a leg, or perhaps two arms, as collectors' items.

BATTLE HYMNS

At Invercargill Canada proudly stood to attention while their imaginatively named national anthem 'O Canada' was played. This was a luxury not afforded them when they met Ireland. At Lansdowne Road, Dublin, the Irish play the republican anthem, 'The Soldiers' Song', but away from home they like to be more cosmopolitan. Against Wales, a tinny version of the 'Rose of Tralee', which sounded as if it had been recorded by James Last, fought a losing battle against the gale force wind that whips through the Athletic Ground in Wellington.

For the game against Canada, Ireland decided they would go without a battle hymn. The organizers decided that if that was the case the anthem of Canada wouldn't be played either. The Canadians were reduced to singing 'O Canada' in their dressing room, and on the field both countries had to stand to attention for 'God Defend New Zealand'. It was a superfluous prayer.

David Lange did not join in the singing of the New Zealand anthem, but then he did not join in anything. The Prime Minister shunned the World Cup because he had not forgiven the New Zealand Rugby Union for turning a blind eye to the Cavaliers' tour to South Africa. The official programme should have included messages of support from the Prime Ministers of Australia and New Zealand.

The familiar coiffured visage of Bob Hawke was there, but in place of Lange we had the unfamiliar balding features of Mike Moore, who turned out to be the New Zealand Minister of Sport.

Lange said he would not attend any of the games. 'Good,' said a NZRU official. 'It will mean three more seats for other people.' Lange weighs 22 stone.

MON DÉSIR

Jacques Chirac, the Prime Minister of France, was less reticent, despite his country's dust-up with New Zealand over the sinking of the Rainbow

Warrior in Auckland Harbour. France, of course, were being typically French on and off the field. They had an incentive to score on the field and a natural urge to score off it. Monsieur Chirac promised the players a three-day sojourn in Tahiti if they reached the quarter-finals and five days for reaching the final. Presumably they could have had the Arc de Triomphe if they had won the Cup, and perhaps seven days in Haiti if they had failed to qualify for the final rounds.

In Auckland the French team stayed at an hotel called Mon Désir and they took the name to heart. Apart from being refused entry to Auckland's latest nightclub because they were dressed in jeans, albeit designer ones, the French availed themselves of the local facilities, not to mention the local women, to such an extent that the management cracked down.

At the Mon Désir the players were confined to their own bar in an attempt to give temptation the hand off. Goodness knows what would have happened had France not beaten Australia in that memorable semi-final in Sydney. As it was, the French themselves contrived to rain on their parade. Jacques Fouroux, the coach and *le petit dictateur*, made a passing reference at the after-match press conference to the fact that his team had been written off by the French press. At that point one of the leading rugby writers in France shot to his feet, shouted at Fouroux and stalked out. Fouroux shouted back, shot to his feet and he, too, then slammed out of the room. End of press conference.

There were other people who felt like walking out at various stages of the competition.

DISINFORMATION ON QUALIFICATION

Bill McLaren, the finest advertisement for Rugby Union since Webb Ellis, found himself announcing that Gavin Hastings had scored 19 points for Scotland against Rumania, when in fact he had scored 21. When Hastings reached the then world record of 27 (it was surpassed an hour and a half later by Didier Camberabero) the television commentary had it as 25.

McLaren, the most meticulous of operators who does his own homework, had a New Zealand television statistician thrust upon him to do

'McLaren had a New Zealand television statistician thrust upon him to do the arithmetic.'

the arithmetic. Out of courtesy to the host broadcasters, McLaren accepted the arrangement.

President Reagan was also misled, as were the Argentinians. In the American Eagles' tour booklet the President wrote: 'All the countries can be proud of the dedication and excellence they have exhibited in qualifying for this championship.' In fact there was no qualification and the 16 competing nations were simply invited.

The Argentinian brochure displayed a map of the world which was coloured brown with Argentinian territory highlighted in dark blue. The Falklands were in dark blue.

Mark Ella, the former Wallaby stand off, who was commentating for Australian television, wasn't so much misled as waylaid. Asked about a specific Japanese player, Ella said: 'I can't tell the difference. They all look the same to me.'

Tim Glover
The Independent